POTTERY DECORATION

POTTERY DECORATION

BY THOMAS SHAFER

WATSON-GUPTILL PUBLICATIONS/NEW YORK

(Frontis) Stoneware bottle, 13½" high. China, Tz'u-chou, Sung dynasty (960–1127 A.D.) The Cleveland Museum of Art, Purchase, J.H. Wade Fund. The graceful, flowing stylized peony design is the perfect complement to the full, round, quiet form. The piece was coated with white, then black slip, the decoration cut through the black exposing the white.

First published 1976 in the United States and Canada by Watson-Guptill Publications,
a division of Billboard Publications, Inc.,
1515 Broadway, New York, N.Y. 10036

Library of Congress Cataloging in Publication Data
Shafer, Thomas, 1937–
Pottery decoration.
Bibliography: p.
Includes index.
1. Pottery craft. 2. Decoration and ornament.
3. Glazes. I. Title.
TT920.S5 1976 738.1'4 75-45355
ISBN 0-8230-4206-5

Manufactured in U.S.A.

First Printing, 1976
6 7 8 9/86 85

Edited by Sarah Bodine
Designed by Bob Fillie
Set in 10 pt. Baskerville

To Yvonne

CONTENTS

PREFACE

Although sometimes thought of as an unnecessary or superfluous added element, decoration can form an integral part of a pot, equal in importance to the form itself in the total esthetic statement.

An essential quality of successful decoration is appropriateness, a special affinity for the form which it enriches. Good decoration need not be subordinate to the form but should enhance it. This may be accomplished in many ways ranging from subtle echoing of the form to bold contrast with it. Unusual, audacious, even incongruous decoration can be exciting when it is done with the assurance and authority which gives it a feeling of rightness, however unexpected.

A form which has little excitement unadorned may become memorable through inspired decoration; but it is equally possible to ruin the most vibrant, powerful form through insensitive decoration. Decoration may be conceived as an integral part of the form before it is even made, or the same form may be decorated in a hundred different equally valid ways. Most producing potters make pots in groups or series, and many almost identical pieces are given individuality through variations in decoration.

In pottery of some periods in history, the form and decoration are inseparable. The exuberant decoration of some Japanese Jomon ware actually seems to create the form. In pottery of the Han dynasty in China, decoration is subtle, simple, only accenting the austere dignity of the forms, yet the ridges, delicate incising, or richly modeled lugs or handles are important parts of the whole and without them the pots would lack much of their vigor and excitement. Although the best pots are usually those in which form and decoration are balanced in an inseparable unity, the decoration in some periods became dominant and the pots are memorable for their embellishment rather than their basic form. In Hispano-Moresque ware many of the forms are more or less neutral backgrounds for lavish decoration. In Renaissance Italy this approach was sometimes carried to an extreme in which pictorial decoration completely ignored the form. In contrast, the pictorial decoration on classical Greek pottery remains subordinate to, and harmonizes with, the strong uncompromising forms.

Successful decoration may be beautiful in itself, as in Spanish medieval lusterware or Ming porcelain, or it may be meaningless apart from the pot it embellishes. It may be as simple as a few calligraphic brushstrokes on a Hamada pot, or as elaborate and incredibly delicate as the blue-and-white ware of 17th-century China, or the French, German, and Dutch work which imitated it. It may be as

Kutani dish. White porcelain decorated in overglaze enamels, 4½" high, 18" in diameter. Japanese, Edo period, 17th century. Freer Gallery of Art, Washington, D.C.

Luster-painted bowl, 11" in diameter. Alan Caiger-Smith, England, 1973. The superbly eloquent brush decoration is in dark, silvery luster over a white tin glaze, grayed in the reduction firing of the luster.

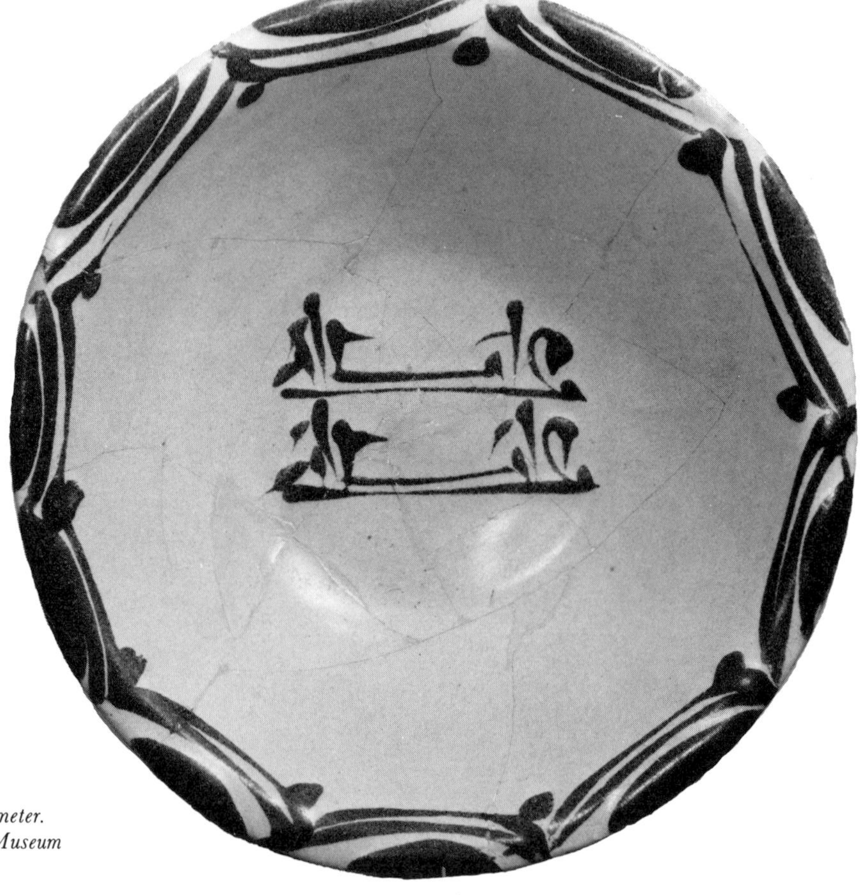

Earthenware bowl, tin-glazed blue on white, 8" in diameter. Mesopotamia, 10th–11th century. The Metropolitan Museum of Art, Harris Brisbane Dick Fund, 1963.

subtle and precise as the delicate incising of a Sung dynasty celadon bowl or as bold, casual, and rough as the brushwork on 17th-century Oribe ware of Japan.

This book deals with the immense variety of materials and techniques which may be employed for the enrichment of clay and glaze surfaces, including decoration in the forming process, carved, impressed, and added decoration, and various methods of using slips, underglaze and overglaze colors, and lusters. The illustrations show tools and processes, as well as pots in museum collections and work by contemporary potters, selected to show various ways in which the techniques discussed have been used.

I would like to express my gratitude to all the potters who generously loaned photographs and especially to John Glick for helping with special photograph requests. Photographs on pages 38 and 39 are by Russ Munn, pages 12, 13, 19, 116, 138 and 139 by Bob Vigiletti, page 15 by George Crary, and page 16 by Evon Streetman. Line drawings are by the author.

I would like to thank all the museums which have supplied excellent photographs and granted permission to reproduce them, and the Fogg Museum, Yale University Art Gallery, the Cleveland Museum, and the Freer Gallery of Art for the privilege of examining pieces not on exhibition. I am especially grateful to Dr. George Lee of Yale and Martin Amt of the Freer for their assistance.

I am indebted to Jim McKinnell, John Glick, and Elly and Willy Kuch, from whom I have learned much about pottery decoration and whose work has been an example and an inspiration. I am also grateful to Jim McKinnell and Victor Spinski for reading portions of the manuscript.

I would like to thank the editors at Watson-Guptill: Donald Holden, with whom the original concept of the book was developed, Diane Hines, and especially Sarah Bodine, with whose assistance this concept took final form.

Finally, warmest thanks must go to my wife, Yvonne, for her enthusiasm, advice, and encouragement through every stage of the process and for typing successive revisions of the manuscript.

Porcelain plate. China, Ting ware, Sung dynasty. Freer Gallery of Art, Washington, D.C. The ultimate in subtle elegance is here achieved with simplicity and restraint. The carved decoration is sharp, precise, yet lively, the glaze a warm ivory.

PART ONE
SCULPTURAL DECORATION

ONE

THE FORMING PROCESS

A decorative surface on a pot may be the unintentional result of a natural, unaffected fabricating process, or a conscious emphasizing or exploitation of that process for decorative effect. A clearly revealed forming process or structure as decoration can be an integral part of the original conception of a pot, with a particular process chosen as a means of achieving a certain decorative effect. A pot can be considered to be completely decorated using any of the techniques discussed in this chapter; however, such things as throwing marks and slab joints are more often subordinate to other decorative treatments.

THROWING AND TRIMMING MARKS

The rhythmic spiral grooves and ridges that result from throwing give pots made on the wheel a unique character. The throwing marks of a skilled potter tend to vary naturally with the kind of pot—deeper and stronger on large or casual pieces, finer and more delicate on small, thin, refined pots. Throwing marks can be exploited by consciously varying their character for different kinds of pots, or even on a single pot to accent a part of the form. The throwing marks on a bottle might, for instance, change from deep and vigorous at the bottom to smoothly rippling on the shoulder to sharp and crisp on the neck. But such variation can easily be carried too far. It must seem natural and unforced, with a logical relationship to the form, or the technique degenerates into meaningless exhibitionism.

Trimming marks, too, may vary but are usually most pleasing when simply and cleanly cut, the tool held at an angle at which it shaves rather than scrapes the pot. Deeply grooved trimming is usually distracting and inappropriate, but in some cases it can be effective.

Porcelain creamer/sugar, showing strong throwing marks, fired to cone 12 with a clear glaze. Jim Makins, U.S.A., 1975.

Coil-built stoneware bottle. Julie Larson, U.S.A. Collection of Melvin Maxwell Smith. The coils (really narrow flattened strips in this case) are built up in closely packed irregular layers resembling the strata of an exposed rock face.

COIL BUILDING

There are two basically different approaches to coil building. The first uses the coils as elements of structure, allowing them to retain their individual identity even though they are flattened, squeezed, or tooled as they are joined together. A richly textured surface, beautifully expressive of its forming process, can be achieved by building with quite soft coils. Each coil is thinned and securely joined To the one below it by a rhythmic squeezing between thumb and fingers, which results in a methodically dimpled surface accented by the wavy lines of the joints.

Coil structures do not necessarily have to be built up in a neat spiral or layer on layer; various patterns can be built in. Although it may be difficult to build complex patterns into free-standing pieces, it is easy when done inside a press mold. Plaster molds are best, as the clay releases from them easily; porous wood is almost as good; and ceramic, metal, or plastic forms may be used if lined with paper towels to prevent the clay from sticking to them. Coils can be laid into the mold in free patterns, filling in with other coils which are then securely joined by pressing and smoothing over the inside (on the side against the mold surface, of course, the pattern remains distinct). The same technique can be used over hump molds, with the inside retaining the pattern and the outside being pressed and smoothed over.

The other approach to coil building uses the coils (often fatter and softer than in the first approach) only as a means of building a rough basic structure, to be formed and refined by squeezing, stretching, scraping, or paddling. In this technique, the individual coils disappear in the process. The coil-built pottery of primitive societies often has surface decoration which is the result of paddling with a wooden beater to thoroughly join the coils, thin and compress the wall, and refine the form, the wall being supported from inside by a wood block that acts as an anvil. The wooden beater, or paddle, wrapped with straw matting, fabric, or cord, or carved with simple or intricate designs, impresses a complex but casual pattern or texture. The technique is still used today in some traditional potteries in Japan and Southeast Asia.

Coil patterns can be laid out with great freedom if a form is used, so that the structure need not be self-supporting during assembly. Here a wood bowl is used as a hump mold.

The outside is pressed and scraped to seal the coils together, but the pattern remains unmarred on the inside. A paper-towel lining is used here to prevent the clay from sticking to the wood mold.

Porcelain bowl, delicately modeled and pierced rim, pale-green copper glaze with blushes of red. Nan McKinnell, U.S.A.

SLAB CONSTRUCTION

Slab construction can be exploited in many ways for decorative effects, both in the way in which the slabs are made and in the manner of joining them together. Slabs can be formed from small units or poured. Each method produces different decorative surfaces. Joints can be left exposed, even emphasized, and the paddling which seals them and refines the form can also pattern the surface.

Pressed Slabs. Slabs made by pressing a mass of clay to the desired thickness with a rolling pin or slab rolling machine, or by pounding with the hand or a wooden paddle, are impressed with the texture of the surface on which they are made. Concrete, wood, burlap, and canvas are good, as they produce distinctive textures and the clay does not stick to their porous surfaces. Impressed patterns and textures are discussed in more detail in Chapter 3.

Using a rolling pin or slab roller, openwork slabs can be made by pressing together pieces of clay of various shapes (strips, coils, slabs, dabs), leaving occasional gaps or spaces, or by laying out grid or lattice patterns. The results are usually more organic than can be achieved with piercing (discussed later). A single slab may be conceived and made as an entity, needing only some forming to become a finished piece, or it may be used as a component in a more complex construction.

Openwork slabs can be formed by pressing together smaller slabs, strips, or dabs. The pattern is first laid out as shown, then rolled with a rolling pin or slab roller to seal joints and flatten the slab.

The stoneware tray at right was formed from one slab. The lattice patterns were embellished with stamping and incising and the piece further decorated with slips and oxide decoration over the raw glaze. John Glick, U.S.A., 1974.

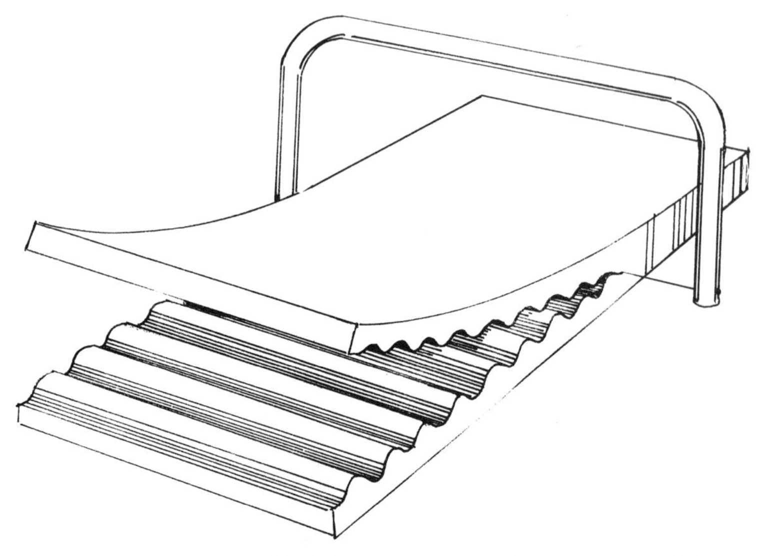

A taut wire can be used to cut slabs with sculptural faces such as the zigzag pattern shown. The cutting is most easily controlled when the wire is held under tension in a steel frame.

Sliced Slabs. Slabs can be made by slicing through a large, well-wedged block of clay with a taut wire or cord. A braided wire leaves a distinct pattern, which although limited to straight parallel lines or some form of wave or shell pattern, can have considerable variety. Similar, but much deeper and stronger, patterns can be made using a stretched-out electric-coil heating element or thin coil spring. It is usually more practical to cut only one side of a slab in this way, cutting the other side with a normal wire.

In using grooved slabs to construct cylindrical forms an effect like very free and fluid fluting is obtained. The slabs can be cut with a stretched-out wire coil or by making a zigzag cut with a straight, taut wire. The first way is easier and produces a regular pattern; the second is more difficult to control, but may give delightfully erratic results.

These 10″ diameter slabs were cut with a stretched-out coil spring about ⅛″ in diameter.

Marbled and Mosaic Slabs. Slabs with marbled or mosaic patterns can be formed from clays of two or more contrasting colors provided they have the same shrinkage rates and maturing temperatures. The clays should be quite soft when joined, as using slip to seal the joints might smear the patterns. The pieces may be dampened with a wet sponge, but this is not necessary if the clays are soft enough and are well pressed together.

Marbled patterns are easy to obtain, but the effects are to some extent a matter of chance. Swirling patterns can be made by stacking up alternating slices of contrasting colored clays, then briefly wedging the mass in the Japanese spiral manner. A different kind of pattern can be obtained by cutting across the layers and recombining the slices.

Checkered or striped patterns can be made with square or rectangular sections of contrasting colors pressed together, then sliced transversely. Complex patterns can be made by assembling simple units. Sandwiches of several thin layers of different colors can be rolled or folded over to make spiral or zigzag patterns. These are then sliced and pressed together on a flat surface to form patterned slabs, or pressed into or onto plaster or wood molds to form pots directly.

Cracking along the joints during drying or firing is almost certain with this technique if the pieces are not very carefully and firmly pressed together. It is difficult to seal joints with slip without smearing the patterns, but the edges of individual slices may be dampened by lightly pressing them against a wet sponge.

(Above) A great variety of simple and complex patterns can be made with strips or slices of contrasting colored clays pressed together, then sliced transversely.

(Left) Slices cut from patterned loaves of contrasting colored clays are arranged, then carefully pressed together in a paper-towel-lined wooden bowl.

Mosaic slab box. Wilhelm and Elly Kuch, W. Germany, 1974. The top of the box is made from a checkered slab, the bottom from a marbled slab, both of brown and white clays.

Poured Slabs. Casting slip can be used to pour slabs onto large plaster bats (see illustration). Color decoration and openwork or relief designs can easily be incorporated into the slabs as they are poured. Decoration in a contrasting slip color can be poured or trailed (discussed in Chapter 6) over the still-wet slab so that it sinks into the surface, or the decoration can be poured directly onto the plaster bat, followed immediately by pouring the slab before the decoration stiffens.

Openwork tracery designs of great complexity and delicacy can be poured, but they may be quite fragile and difficult to handle in construction. Shallow, openwork bowls can be trailed directly into plaster press molds. Relief patterns can be trailed onto slightly stiffened, but still-wet, slabs.

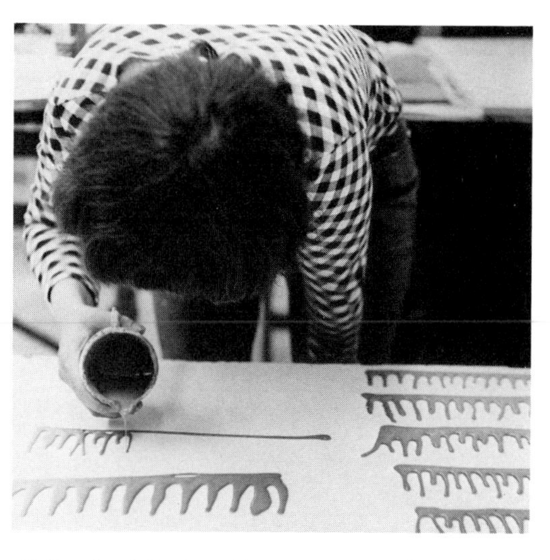

Deflocculated slip poured in patterns onto a plaster slab will stiffen to form slabs. The pours shown here are intended for a sculptural construction.

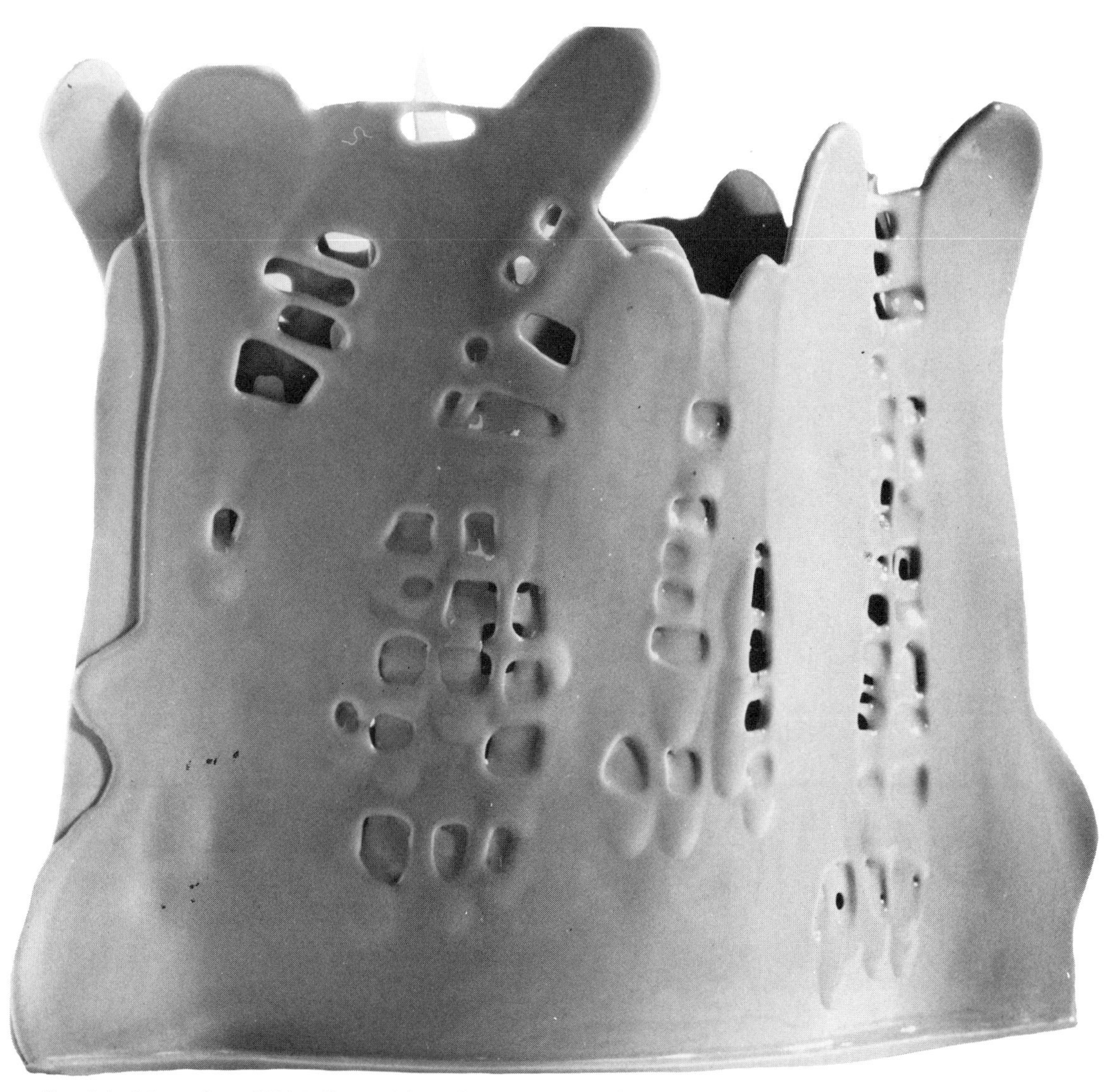

Porcelain slab vase form, 8" high. Kurt and Gerda Spurey, Austria, 1973. This fluidly graceful, yet crisply dynamic envelope form is constructed of very thin poured porcelain slabs. The lattice patterns, as well as the lobed top edge, were created in the pouring process.

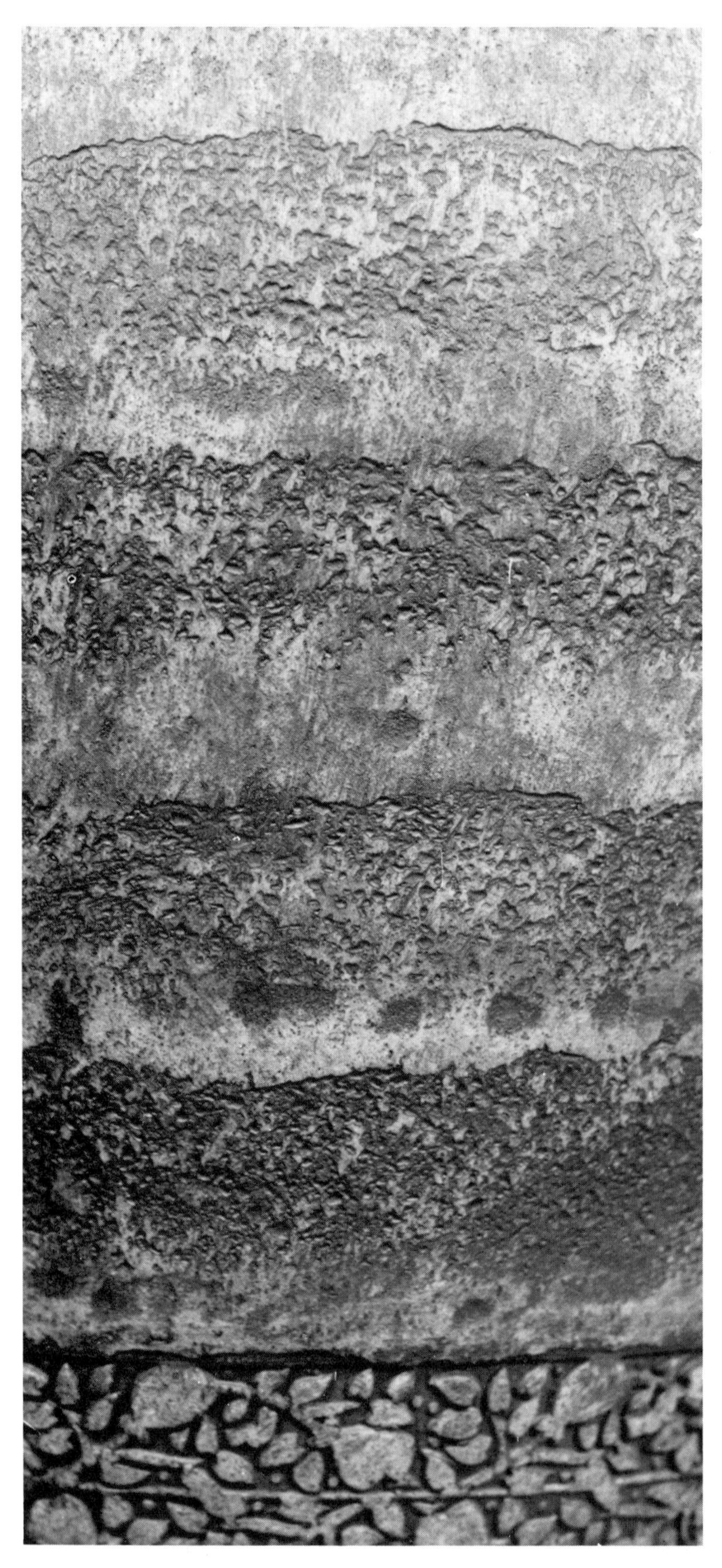

Detail of large slab-built bottle, by the author, 1973. Paddling to secure joints and refine the form has reduced the visible edges of the lapped joints to lines and almost, but not quite, erased the finger marks resulting from squeezing the slabs together as they were joined. Most of the pitted texture impressed by the concrete on which the slabs were made has been preserved.

Deflocculants. To minimize shrinkage, and to avoid warping and cracking problems, a deflocculated slip should be used for poured slabs. By adding a deflocculant, only about half as much water is needed to wet the clay particles to a fluid consistency, which substantially decreases the amount of shrinkage as the water evaporates. Because of electrical attraction, clay grains normally form clumps, or flocks, in water so that an amount of water almost equal in weight to that of the dry body ingredients is required to make a pourable slip. A small amount of a deflocculant, such as sodium silicate or soda ash (about ½ per cent by weight of the dry ingredients), tends to break up the clumps, so that each grain is completely surrounded by water, giving the slip a fluid, syrupy consistency, using only 40 to 50 parts water to 100 parts dry ingredients. The deflocculant also holds the clay particles in suspension longer.

Sodium silicate is made by calcining soda ash and is commercially available in a solution commonly known as waterglass. In industry, a mixture of soda ash and sodium silicate is normally used; with fairly plastic clay bodies, a half-and-half mixture works well. The deflocculants must be completely dissolved in the water before adding the dry ingredients, which should be added slowly while stirring constantly. The slip must be thoroughly mixed and sieved to eliminate any lumps, and, ideally, should be allowed to stand covered for 24 hours before using.

Not all clay bodies can be successfully deflocculated. Porcelain and light stoneware bodies usually work well, while clays with a high iron content may be unsatisfactory. Some experimentation is necessary to determine the ideal proportions of water and deflocculant for a particular clay body. If more than one part deflocculant or 50 parts water to 100 parts dry ingredients by weight is required to achieve the proper fluidity, the body will not make a good pouring slip. Only the minimum amount of deflocculant necessary should be used, as too much may make the slip gel. Also, sodium silicate and soda ash, when dissolved in the water and absorbed into the plaster, gradually seal up the pores of the plaster so that it eventually loses its porosity and its usefulness.

As plasticity is not an important quality in slip casting, commercial casting bodies normally have a high proportion (often more than 50%) of nonplastic ingredients to cut down shrinkage. Poured slabs used for building pots, however, need reasonable plasticity, and a normal handbuilding or throwing body, properly deflocculated, may be ideal.

Slab Joints. Just as in wood construction, where beautifully dovetailed or pegged joints may be decorative as well as functional, exposed joints in clay slab construction can be exploited as embellishments of a pot. They are also an index of the skill of the craftsman, for a good joint must be surely and deftly made, though not necessarily smoothly finished. Rough, spontaneous joining with ragged edges suits the character of some pots, while on others the joint may appear as an incised line in a smooth surface. Labored or fussy joints are better smoothed over and hidden. The type of joint, butted or overlapped, and the way in which it is sealed together by pressing or squeezing with the fingers, tooling, or paddling produce a wide variety of effects. Exposed joints may be a straightforward articulation of a purely practical assembly of the parts or they may be planned to accent the form or to make a pattern. Exploitation of slab structure as decoration may easily be carried to excess, however, with overelaboration of the joints or their forced, unnatural arrangement, perverting structure as decoration into decoration masquerading as structure.

Unglazed gray pottery jar. China, 10″ high. Late Chou period, ca. 600–222 B.C. The Cleveland Museum of Art, Purchase, J. H. Wade Fund. The surface texture is a result of beating with a patterned wood paddle.

CARVED DECORATION

Carving includes a wide range of techniques and effects, from simple scratched lines to elaborate sculptural relief and pierced decoration, that can be achieved with a variety of cutting tools. Although it is not a carving technique, wax-resist etching is also included in this chapter, as the result is similar.

INCISING

Incising is perhaps the oldest and most natural method of decoration. Simple linear patterns cut or scratched into soft or leatherhard clay appear on some of the earliest pots of various cultures in Europe, Asia, Africa, and the Americas. Mesopotamian pottery with incised decoration, dating between 5000 and 4500 B.C., has been found at sites in Iraq and Syria. Carved decoration reached a peak of subtle, elegant perfection in Sung dynasty China. The designs, usually stylized floral patterns, are sometimes very simple, with only a few graceful incised lines—in Ting ware they are often so delicate as to be barely visible under a smooth ivory-colored glaze. On the northern celadons the decoration is often quite complex, with the background beveled around intricate flower and petal shapes, causing the rich, translucent gray-green or olive-green glaze to pool and become darker in the depressions so that the decoration seems to float on the surface. The incising in both types is sharp, crisp, and clean, yet graceful and flowing.

Incised decoration is most often done on leatherhard pots, but depending on the tools used, the type of incising, and personal preferences, the ware may be considerably softer or harder. Except in quite hard clay, drawing with a simple, sharp-pointed tool leaves a ridge, or burr, along the line like a plowed furrow, which when fired can be unpleasantly rough or sharp. A chisel-shaped point or a wire loop tool actually removes the clay instead of plowing it. Excising areas around a linear pattern is easily done with a knife, one of the many kinds of wire or spring-steel loop tools, or a Japanese-type trimming tool made from a piece of banding steel. Incising should not be too deep (1/8″ or less is usually enough) unless the piece is quite large and thickwalled. Incised lines deeper than half the wall thickness will weaken the structure and may even cause cracking.

Earthenware urn. Japanese, middle Jomon. Freer Gallery of Art, Washington, D.C.

After outlining the design with a pointed wooden tool or pencil, a wire loop tool can be used to excise negative areas, leaving the pattern raised above the background.

Stoneware bottle, slab built with thrown neck, 24" high, by the author, 1973.

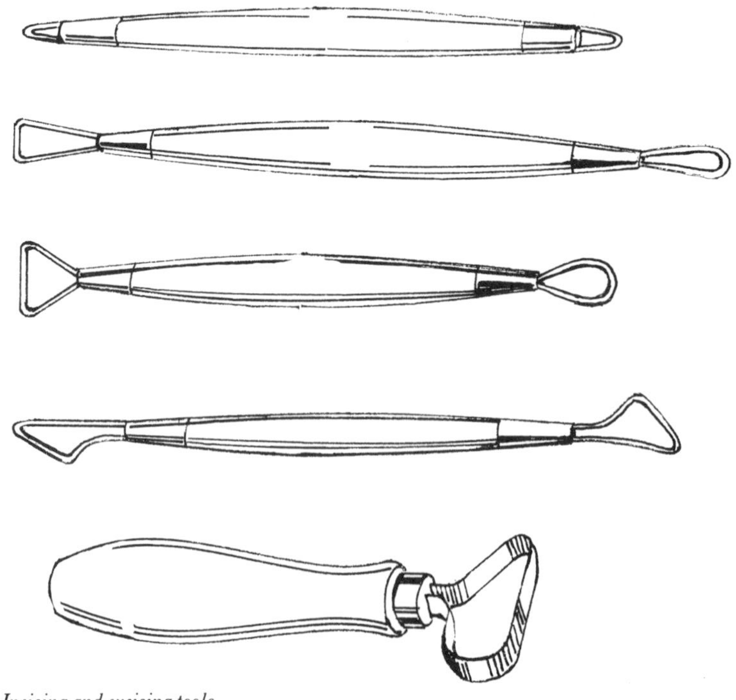

Incising and excising tools

Stoneware vase. China, Tz'u-chou ware, Sung dynasty. Freer Gallery of Art, Washington, D.C. A coating of white slip is cut through to expose the gray body which is itself deeply carved. The lush swirling plant forms of the decoration are in complete harmony with the exaggerated curves of the form, but both form and decoration have a clear, crisp quality which gives the piece as much dignity as it has voluptuousness.

Stoneware bottle. Wilhelm and Elly Kuch, Germany, 1974, light-brown clay, iron-oxide wash, unglazed except for inside and neck. The whimsical stylized landscape was spontaneously drawn in the soft clay; the parallel lines at the bottom were incised with a fork.

Slab-built bottle. Petr Svoboda, Czechoslovakia. The crisp linear geometric pattern, inscribed with straight edge and compass, contrasts beautifully with the coarse clay body.

(Opposite page) Earthenware vase. China, Shang dynasty. Freer Gallery of Art, Washington, D.C. Uncompromising in its formal rigidity (influenced by contemporary bronze vessels) the decoration, though carefully fitted to the swelling form, seems basically in conflict with it. Yet this incongruity makes the pot more fascinating and memorable than many with more appropriate decoration.

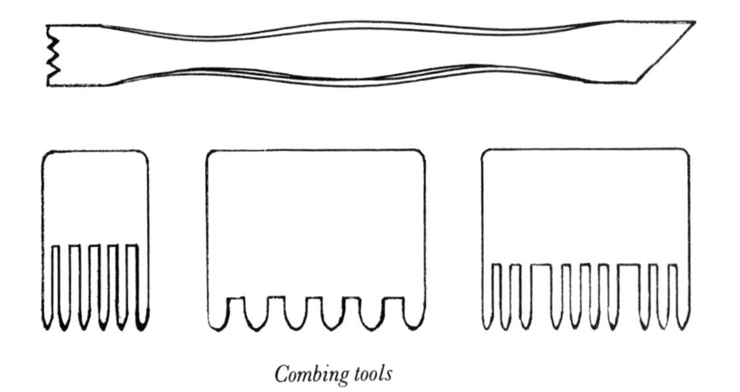

Combing tools

COMBING

Combing is often used as a kind of filler or embellishment in an incised design, but it can also be used alone for fast, simple patterns. Narrow combs with only a few (5 to 10) teeth are easily manipulated on curved surfaces; wide combs are somewhat unwieldy except for broad effects on flat surfaces. Sections of ordinary wood or plastic hair combs, or dinner forks, can be used as combing tools. Combs can also be cut from thin wood or plastic.

Celadon porcelain bowl. China, Sung dynasty. The Cleveland Museum of Art, The Fanny Tewksbury King Collection. This elegant small bowl is simply decorated with a lightly incised floral design accented with combing.

FACETING

Faceting is a method of altering the shape of a round pot by cutting or shaving the wall to create a multisided form. A variety of tools may be used for this, from a fettling knife to a clay plane. With practice it is possible to cut very clean, accurate facets with a simple knife, but some potters prefer to use one of the many types of slicing tools which can be purchased, made, or improvised. One of the most popular and easiest to find is the type of cheese slicer with a wire cutter and a thin roller guide. This will shave very straight, even facets, the depth of cut being determined by the angle at which the cutter is held. Pots for faceting must have thicker than normal walls, the thickness increasing as the number of cut faces decreases (the fewer the facets, the deeper the cuts must be to make them uniform). In some cases it may be necessary to lightly paddle the pot into a polygonal form before cutting the facets.

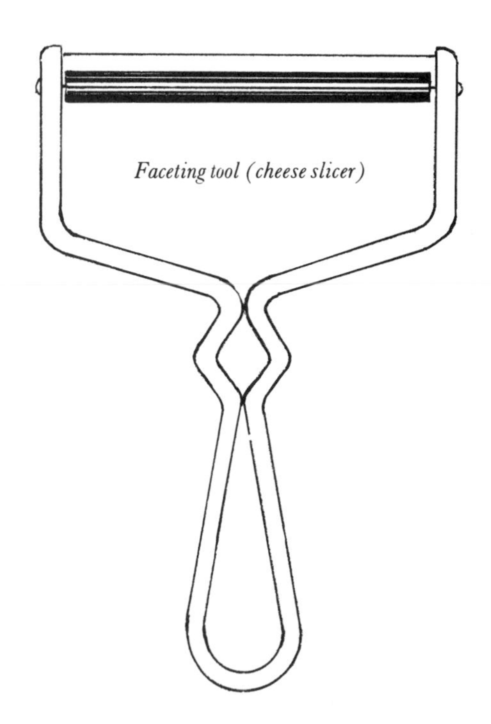

Faceting tool (cheese slicer)

Faceted porcelain jar. David Shaner, U.S.A., 1973.

Salt-glazed fluted vase. Rochester Folk Art Guild, U.S.A. The break in the vertical fluting in the center adds a subtle grace to the severely simple form and decoration.

FLUTING

Very subtle, delicate fluting was done by Sung dynasty Chinese potters; the shallow, parallel grooves are usually vertical, but they are sometimes curved or diagonal to create a spiral effect. Fluting is most easily done on cylindrical forms, but it can be very beautiful on spherical or hemispherical forms such as bottles, jars, or bowls.

Fluting should be done when the pot is soft, but firm enough to be handled. A smooth, fine-textured body is best—the technique is most often used with porcelain. A spring-steel or wire loop tool may be used, but it is easier to maintain a uniform groove depth with the type of Japanese-type homemade tool used by Bernard Leach. To make the tool, a hole (¼″ to ½″ diameter) is drilled about 1″ from the end of a thin, flat piece of soft metal (e.g., strap steel or aluminum) about 1″ wide and 6″ long. The rim of the hole is flared, using a ballpeen hammer; then the long end of the tool is clamped in a vise with about half the hole covered, and the short end is bent to a 45° angle. The cutting edge of the hole is sharpened with a round file, and the tool is ready to use.

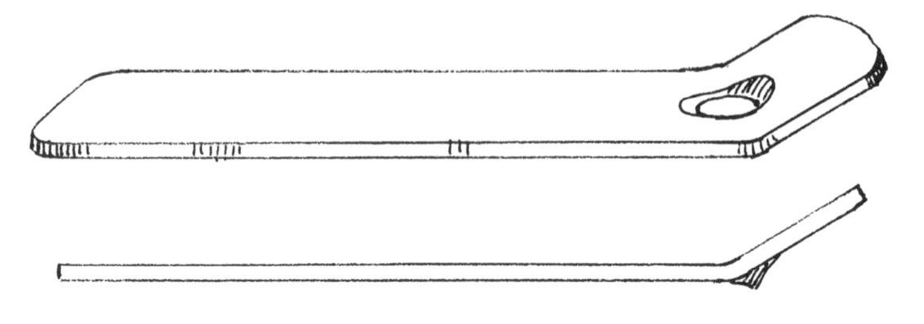

Fluting tool (top and side views)

Fluted stoneware vase. China, Sung dynasty, Freer Gallery of Art, Washington, D.C. The precise, closely spaced fluting is subtly emphasized by a dark-brown glaze which is lighter where it has run thin on the raised edges.

PIERCING

Incised decoration carried to its logical extreme actually pierces the wall. A few simple apertures may serve to accent an incised design, or the piercing may almost dissolve the wall into an elaborate filigree tracery. In Ming dynasty China, delicate reticulated patterns requiring great skill and patience to successfully execute were called "Kuei Kung" (devil's work).

Pierced decoration may be done on nonfunctional pieces, on those where it does not interfere with function, or on double-walled pieces. In some cases the function may be enhanced by pierced decoration. Air circulating through the sides of a pierced fruit bowl keeps the fruit fresh longer; and the pierced outer wall of a double-walled container for hot liquids, such as a tea bowl, provides a cool grip.

Beautiful double-walled ewers were made in Persia in the 12th century, combining incised and pierced decoration. The incised pattern gives continuity to the pierced areas, which in turn accent the incised design. The pierced holes are small and the inner wall is not really seen. The technique was popular in 17th-century Europe, where it was carried to elaborate extremes of complexity and fragility—sometimes graceful and beautiful, sometimes grotesque. On some pieces a solid inner wall was glazed in a color that contrasted with the pierced outer wall, providing a dramatic background for the delicate fretwork.

Twelfth-century Persian potters achieved wonderful effects by accenting delicately incised decoration with a network of tiny holes. Filled by the translucent glaze with which the pieces were coated, the pierced patterns appear as tiny glowing points of light.

Porcelain bowl, 4½" in diameter. China, Ming dynasty, Yale University Art Gallery, Gift of Dr. Yale Kneeland, Jr. This type of intricate pierced decoration was called Kuei Kung (devil's work) because of the extreme delicacy and patience required to execute it.

The best tool for pierced decoration is a knife with a thin, sharp blade that tapers to a point, such as the potter's fettling knife, although a needle may be preferable for really fine work.

Piercing should be done when the clay is firm, but soft enough to cut easily and cleanly. If the clay is too soft, the cutting is not as clean and the form is easily distorted; if too hard, the cutting is difficult and the piece easily cracked. Holes should be kept small, as large openings tend to destroy the form visually as well as cause warping as the clay dries. Piercing is often a part of an incised or impressed design, but may be used independently.

Pierced decoration has often been done in imitation of latticework, and an alternative, although less structurally sound, method is to cut fairly large openings which are then filled in with an actual lattice of interweaving clay strips or coils. This type of work should be done when the basic form is somewhat softer than leatherhard. Pierced ware should be dried very slowly and carefully to prevent cracking due to uneven shrinkage.

Dies for Piercing. A short section of thin metal tubing can be used to pierce neat, uniform holes in a damp clay wall. Round and square brass tubing can be purchased in various sizes and can easily be bent or pinched into other shapes. Ceramic hobby shops sell tools resembling tiny cookie cutters, complete with plungers for rejecting cutout pieces which tend to stick in the tube.

This technique was used in the 18th century by potters in Leeds, England, to quickly develop quite complex pierced decoration using only a few simple metal dies in various combinations (see illustration).

Piercing tools:

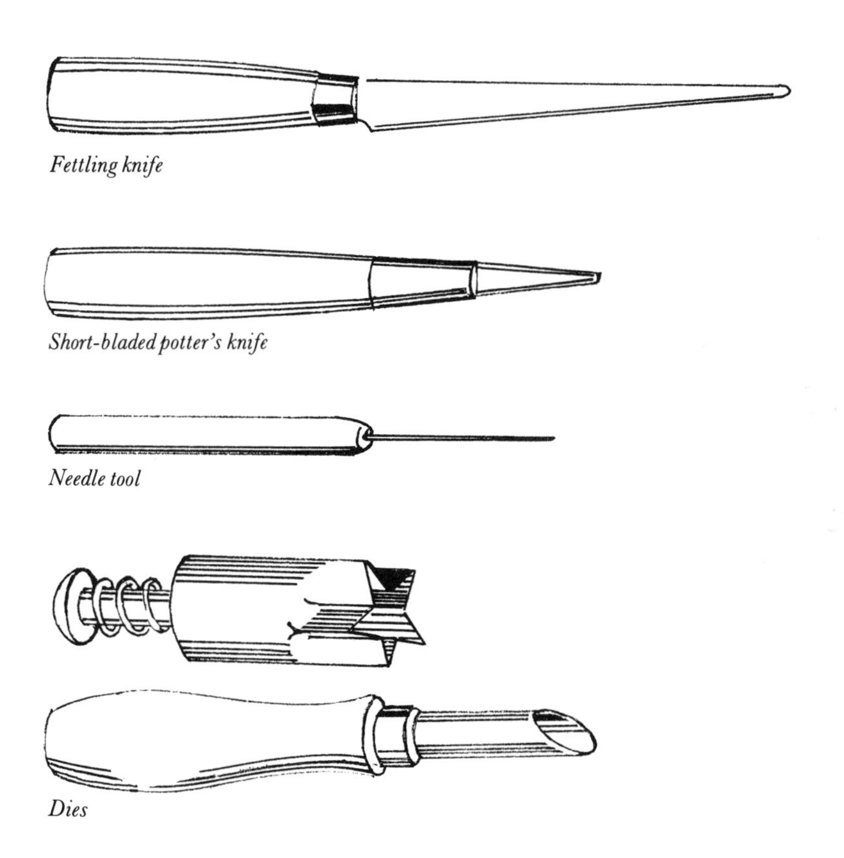

Fettling knife

Short-bladed potter's knife

Needle tool

Dies

The pattern is first drawn in the soft clay with a wooden tool.

A fettling knife is used to cut apertures outlined by the incised pattern.

Stoneware hanging planter. Karl Christiansen, U.S.A., 1975. The incised design is punctuated by the piercing, which in turn is given continuity by the linear pattern. The incised design is emphasized by a glaze which is whiter and more opaque where it gathers in the incisions.

Salt-glazed stoneware mug. Germany. Victoria and Albert Museum. The sprigged medallion is surrounded by incised floral decoration. The bands on the neck and foot were probably made with templates.

TEMPLATES

A decorative rim or band on a wheelthrown pot can be quickly and precisely formed using a rib or template. I prefer to make them of thin wood (⅛″ or less), although plastic or metal could be used. A little extra thickness is left in the rim, foot, or other area where the decorative band is to be. When the form is otherwise completed, the rib (lubricated with water) is held firmly against the pot at it turns on the wheel. If held at a 90° angle to the pot, the template will cut into the clay, but if held at an acute angle it will compress the clay. Either or both ways will work (see illustration).

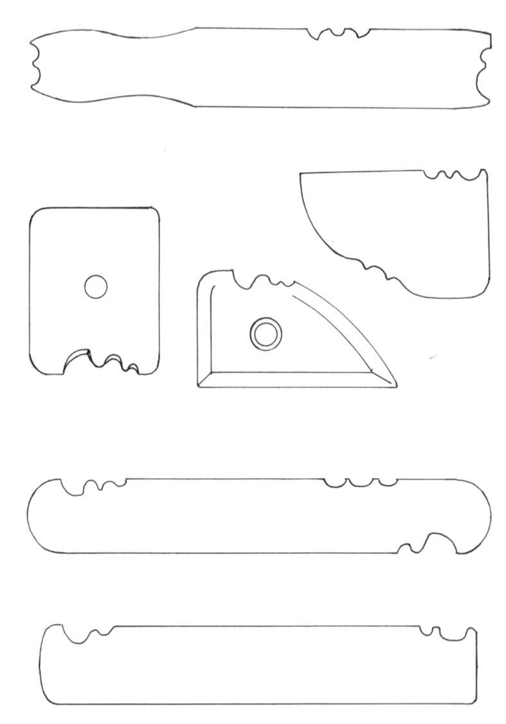

Templates for decorative rims or bands can be made from thin wood such as tongue depressors, paint-stirring paddles, or throwing ribs.

WAX-RESIST ETCHING

This technique is similar to that of etching a metal printing plate. Wax is used to mask areas not to be etched; the etching is done with water.

A wax design is first applied to the leatherhard pot. Hot wax should be used, as water-soluble wax emulsion tends to be washed away by the etching process. (See wax resist in Chapter 6.) A half-and-half mixture of beeswax and paraffin heated to about 200°C. (392°F.) has been found to work well for this technique. When the wax has hardened, the surface is lightly scrubbed with a soft, wet sponge which erodes the unprotected areas, leaving the wax-coated design standing in relief. The scrubbing leaves a coarse, grainy surface as the fine particles are washed away, resulting in a textured contrast which further emphasizes the relief pattern. The scrubbing should be done quickly and without excess water so that the moisture does not soak into the wall and cause cracking. The process can be repeated to develop two or more levels of relief.

A variation of the technique introduces a color contrast as well as surface texture and relief by first coating the pot with a white or colored slip. The wax is applied over the stiffened slip and the scrubbing removes the unprotected areas of the slip coating as well as etching the surface of the pot.

Phil Hargus applies a wax design over a slip-coated leatherhard plate.

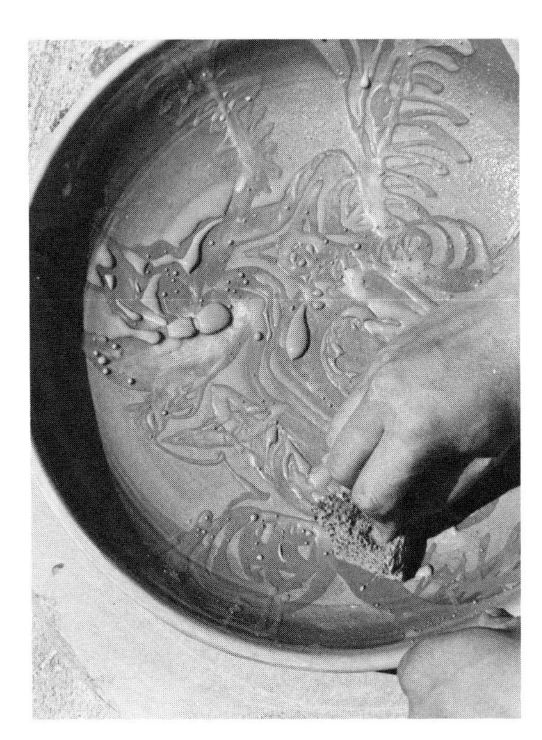

Light scrubbing with a wet sponge removes the slip coating and etches the surface of the pot in the unwaxed areas, leaving the wax-coated areas in relief.

THREE

IMPRESSED DECORATION

Impressing is probably the oldest decorating technique and is certainly one of the easiest and fastest ways to enrich the clay surface. As almost anything harder than soft clay will leave an impression, surfaces of great variety and richness can be made very quickly. However, the very ease and speed of the technique, as well as the great wealth of possibilities, often lead to excess. It is so easy and tempting to overdecorate: sheer quantity, meaningless variety, monotonous repetition, and random jumbles of decoration are equally deadly. Almost the entire surface may be patterned with stamps with beautiful results, but some pots may be best served by only a narrow band or by one small stamp which enlivens the form while remaining completely subordinate. Interesting variety and dramatic contrast can be achieved through the use of different types of stamps on a single piece; but a logical relationship must be maintained among them—and to the pot—to avoid a meaningless profusion of unrelated detail.

USING STAMPS

Porous materials like clay, wood, and plaster are best for stamps as they do not stick to the clay; but nonporous ones, such as metal and plastic, may be used on fairly stiff clay, and the sticking problem is not great if the stamps are small and/or flexible.

The ideal consistency of the clay to be impressed is somewhat stiffer than that used for throwing on the wheel. Before stamping, it is usually advisable to wait until a thrown pot has stiffened somewhat. To get a clear impression and minimize distortion when a stamp is applied, the wall should always be supported from the inside by one hand. The ideal consistency for stamping is the consistency at which slabs can be rolled out without sticking to the rolling pin and can easily be picked up and handled. It is difficult to get a good impression from a large stamp if the clay is too stiff, but small stamps, especially metal ones, work well even on clay which is almost leatherhard.

Stoneware bottle, 10″ high, by the author, 1973. Four small wood stamps were used to impress the decoration in the slab wall before assembly of the pot.

FOUND OR READYMADE STAMPS

Many ordinary objects may be used: faucet handles, screw heads, nuts and bolts, decorative brackets, handles or moldings from old furniture, decorative fragments of buildings, pieces of wood or string, and natural objects such as bark, stones, shells, or even leaves. Readymade stamps include butter or cookie molds, butter paddles and stamps, patterned rolling pins, old wood type, and woodcuts used for printing fabric or wallpaper.

Interesting molds can sometimes be found in gourmet-cooking departments or in antique stores. Used fabric-printing blocks from India are available in a wide variety of delicate and elaborate designs, many of which are ideal for clay. Although some are very small, others are quite large and may need to be pounded with a wood or rubber mallet to obtain a clear, even impression. This obviously can be done only on clay slabs before they are assembled. On some very large blocks, the pattern is made up of several small, independent designs, which may be more useful if cut into several smaller stamps.

Various materials pressed into the clay leave clear impressions. Clockwise from top right on the slab are: machine-crocheted edging, burlap, nylon net, hand-crocheted doily, yew leaf, aluminum grille, crocheted edging, and plastic net.

Indian textile-printing blocks are crisply and cleanly carved from hardwood. Sixteen separate blocks are shown here; some are sections cut from larger complex blocks.

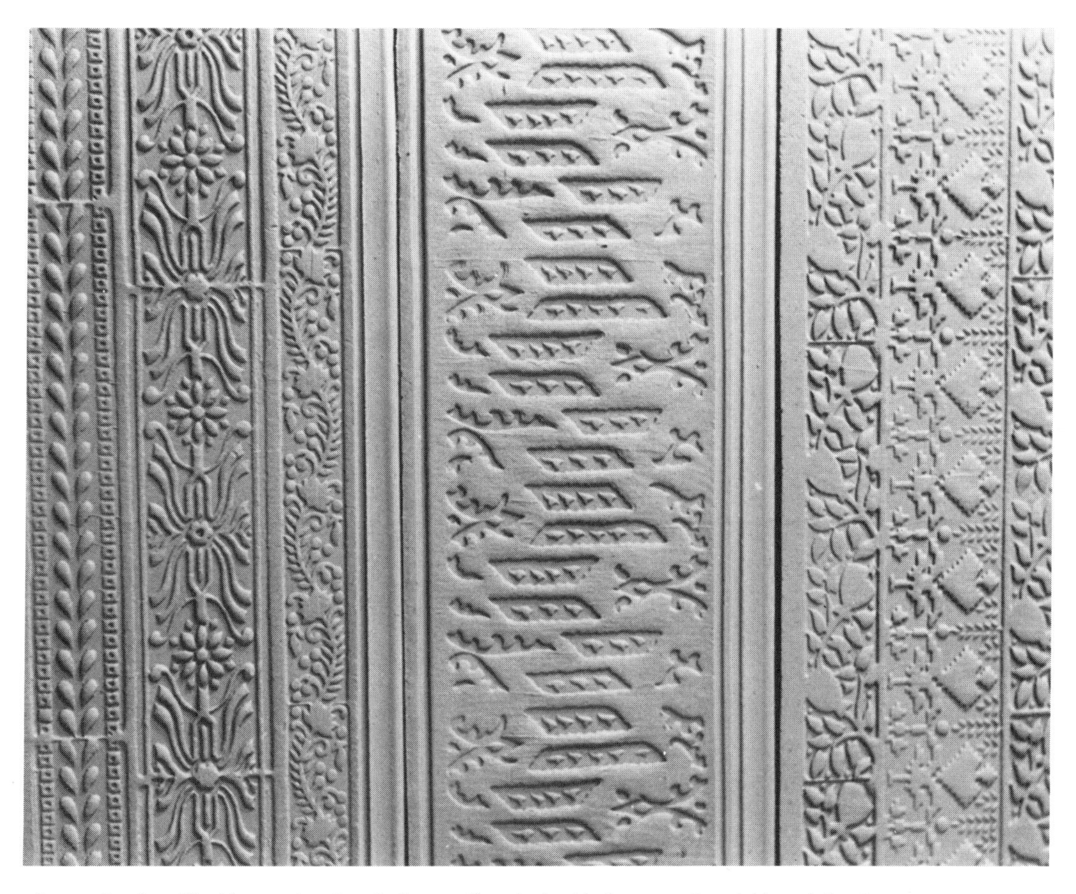

Repeated and combined impressions from Indian textile-printing blocks can produce richly varied surfaces.

IMPRESSING SLABS

Slab construction offers the greatest range of opportunities for impressing the clay surface, because the impressing can be done before the slabs are assembled. Firm, even pressure can be applied to the flat slabs, resulting in clear, even impressions.

The slabs can be rolled or beaten on a surface that impresses its character into the clay. Strongly grained wood, weathered concrete, burlap and other coarsely woven materials, nylon mesh, and corrugated cardboard are some of the possibilities. A pitted texture can be made by pressing into the surface sawdust or coffee grounds, which will burn out in the firing. Flexible metal, plastic, or fiberboard grilles—obtainable at building supply stores—may be pressed onto slabs of clay with a rolling pin for a uniform overall pattern.

NEWS MATS

Impressions can be made from paper fiber news mats or dub sheets, used as molds for making lead printing plates, and regularly discarded by newspapers, which use new mats for printing. Slabs may be pressed directly onto the mats, but the resulting impression will be backwards. To make the impression legible, a plaster cast can be made from the mat. To insure clean separation of the mat from the hardened plaster, the mat should first be coated with a clear plastic spray. A cast can be made of the entire mat and clay slabs then pressed onto it, or small sections (or large ones cut into pieces) can be cast and used as stamps.

Unfortunately this technique lends itself too readily to applications which are trite or cute and is more often exploited for its literal rather than decorative quality.

Vase. Wilhelm and Elly Kuch, Germany. Coarse fabric impressions are enhanced by small added dabs of clay and tiny impressed holes.

CLAY STAMPS

Although beautiful textures and patterns can be made with found or readymade stamps, those which afford the greatest satisfaction to the potter are often those which he makes himself.

Stamps can be made from a variety of materials. The most satisfactory are porous and easy to cut or form: clay, wood, and plaster are the most commonly used. Clay itself is the material most quickly and easily made into stamps, a pattern being cut in the soft or leatherhard state. The only disadvantage is that they must be bisque-fired before being used, although they can be tested by pressing very soft clay onto the stamps when they are a little dryer than leatherhard. Slight alterations can still be made at this time. A clay stamp may itself be a pressing from another object—fired clay, wood, metal, etc.—but the sharpness of the original may be somewhat softened.

PATTERNED MOLDS

Pots can be formed and decorated in the same operation using bisque-fired clay molds decorated with incised or impressed designs. This means making many identical pots to justify the time spent making the molds, but considerable variety can be achieved through added foot rings, pedestals, handles, spouts, etc., by assembling various press-molded sections in different combinations, or through the use of diverse glazes and glazing techniques.

The technique was developed in Hellenistic Greece and widely used by the Romans for making small bowls. Clay was pressed into the decorated mold, the interior of the vessel refined on the potter's wheel while still in the mold, and a foot ring, rim, or handles added after removal from the mold. Decorative motifs were influenced by or copied from contemporary metalwork decoration.

Similar molds were used by Sung dynasty Chinese potters, who pressed clay slabs over convex press molds (hump molds) to make bowls with decoration inside very like that carved in wheelthrown bowls. Although lacking the crispness and spontaneous individuality of the carved decoration, the impressed designs were more complex and minutely detailed.

Thirteen-century Persian potters used two-piece bisque press molds, either carved or stamped directly, or formed from exquisitely carved wood, clay, or plaster master models, to form bowls and more complex jugs and bottles. Some were assembled from press-molded sections. Foot rings, spouts, or handles were normally added rather than being included in the mold.

INSULATING-BRICK STAMPS

Insulating firebrick is very easily cut with metal tools, but sharp, clear lines are impossible because of the crumbly nature of the material. This roughness, however, may be a desirable characteristic for some pots. Manufacturers number the bricks according to the maximum temperature rating, the commonly available numbers being 1620, 2000, 2300, 2600, 2800, and 3000. The lower-temperature bricks (2000 or 2300; 1620 is perhaps too soft) of most brands are fine-textured, soft, and easy to cut; the higher-temperature bricks (2600) are harder and coarser, but crumbly. Still higher-temperature bricks (2800) are very hard, dense, and more difficult to cut, but still rather crumbly.

It is advisable to use old or very cheap tools for cutting insulating bricks; the abrasiveness of the material quickly destroys sawteeth and sharp edges. A cheap saw with large-toothed, replaceable blades is good for cutting the bricks into the desired sizes. A hacksaw blade, a fettling knife, or even nails are useful in making the design. Files and rasps are also very useful, but their sharpness will quickly be dulled by the deceptively soft bricks. It is best to use new bricks rather than used ones, as repeated heating and cooling weakens their structure and makes them more likely to crack or crumble.

PLASTER STAMPS

Plaster can be cast in cardboard tubes or boxes, for small stamps, or in large forms to make bats or molds onto or into which clay can be pressed. Plaster stamps must, of course, be handled more carefully than clay or wood stamps; but reasonably hard, dense, chip-resistant casts may be made from regular potter's plaster by using a high proportion of plaster to water, about 3 to 3¼ pounds per quart. The hardness and density of plaster is determined by the proportion of water with which it is mixed. The proper ratio is usually expressed by the manufacturer in terms of the amount of water by weight to 100 parts plaster by weight. As 1 quart of water weighs about 2.1 pounds, 1 quart of water to 3 pounds plaster would be equivalent to 70 pounds water to 100 pounds plaster, expressed simply as 70. The lower the number, the less fluid the mixture and consequently the harder the cured plaster will be. Each type of plaster has a range of consistency at which it can be used, producing harder casts with less water, softer and more porous casts with more water. The recommended consistency for molding or casting plaster is from 64 to 80.

Harder, more durable casts may be obtained by using commercially available hardener, which is mixed with the water before adding the plaster, or by using one of the many types of especially formulated harder plasters such as Hydrocal, Hydrostone, or Ultracal. These require a much smaller amount of water to set up and produce very hard, smooth casts, but are difficult to carve and, of course, are much less porous.

To mix plaster, the powder is sifted slowly into the water (plaster must always be added to water, never water to plaster), so the water can be absorbed as the plaster is added. A good, medium-density mixture can be achieved without measuring by simply adding plaster slowly to the water until the plaster will no longer settle beneath the surface of the water. When all the plaster has been added, it must be allowed to slake for 2 to 4 minutes; it should then be stirred for a few minutes until the mixture is completely smooth and creamy. It should be poured into the molds when it has just started to thicken but still pours freely. Shake or tap the molds sharply to force out air bubbles. The plaster will solidify very quickly, generating some heat in the process. When it begins to cool (usually in about an hour), it can be removed safely from the mold. Cardboard tubes or boxes used as molds are simply stripped off the hardened plaster.

Designs should be cut into the plaster while it is still damp. About 2 hours after it has set, plaster is hard enough to carve; but it may not harden completely for several days, and may be kept damp indefinitely by wrapping in plastic. After plaster has hardened, it is much more difficult to cut and much more likely to break or chip during carving.

Very precise, clear patterns can be cut in plaster, but very delicate ones are likely to be chipped in use, if not in carving. A few simple tools are sufficient: a pencil, a hacksaw blade, a fettling knife, and a small rasp. The design is first sketched, then it is incised into the plaster with the pencil; lines are widened and deepened with the end of the fettling knife or rasp. Special tools are available to make the work faster, easier, more pleasant, and more precise: these include a great variety of shapes and sizes of gouges, chisels, rasps, and loop tools. Tools for wood- or linoleum-block printing work well, but plaster may dull fine edges. As it is being carved, the stamp can be tested

Stamps carved and cast in plaster; the round stamps are about 2" in diameter.

from time to time in soft clay. When finished, it should be tested again, and the test clay, which will pick up loose crumbs of plaster, discarded.

Plaster stamps or molds can also be made from a clay model or from wood or metal objects. Objects with undercuts should be avoided because they cannot be released from the hardened plaster without breaking the mold. For plaster casting, a design in clay should be quite stiff, even leatherhard. Extremely delicate designs in clay should be avoided—especially thin, deeply incised lines—as it is difficult to get the plaster to fill them because of trapped air; and even if the plaster does fill the spaces properly, the mold will be fragile.

A wall of clay or cardboard is built around the model (1″ to 2″ high for small ones, higher for very large ones) with the bottom edges carefully sealed so the liquid plaster cannot run out. The plaster is poured into the resulting cavity. After the cast has set, the wall is removed and the model should release easily in one piece.

If the model is wood or metal, it must be sized to prevent the plaster from sticking to it. Damp clay does not need sizing because it does not stick to plaster. Commercial soap or silicone sizing is available in ceramic supply houses; petroleum jelly or lard can also be used. Soap sizing can be made by dissolving 1/4 cup of soap flakes or granules (not detergent) in 1 quart of boiling water, then simmering until the mixture is clear.

Clay slabs can be pressed or rolled on large-patterned plaster bats or molds similar to the bisque molds discussed in the section on clay stamps. This is a quick and easy way to decorate large surfaces, but it can become monotonous if used very often; whereas a few small stamps may be combined in many different ways to form large, complex patterns. Large, circular slabs of plaster may be poured in cake pans which have been coated first with sizing. Rectangular forms can easily be set up with four boards on a smooth, nonporous surface (Formica is ideal) with soft clay pressed along their outer edges to hold them in place and prevent plaster from leaking out. The inside faces of the boards should be coated with sizing. When the plaster has set, the wooden forms are simply removed. The thickness necessary for a strong slab may vary from 1″ to 4″, depending on size. The strength can be increased by embedding a layer of burlap in the plaster. Plaster bowl molds can be cast in or over sized plastic, metal, wood, or ceramic bowls, and trimmed on the wheel to alter or refine the form. Amounts of plaster and water required to fill a form can be determined by using a volume of water equal to 5/7 the vol-

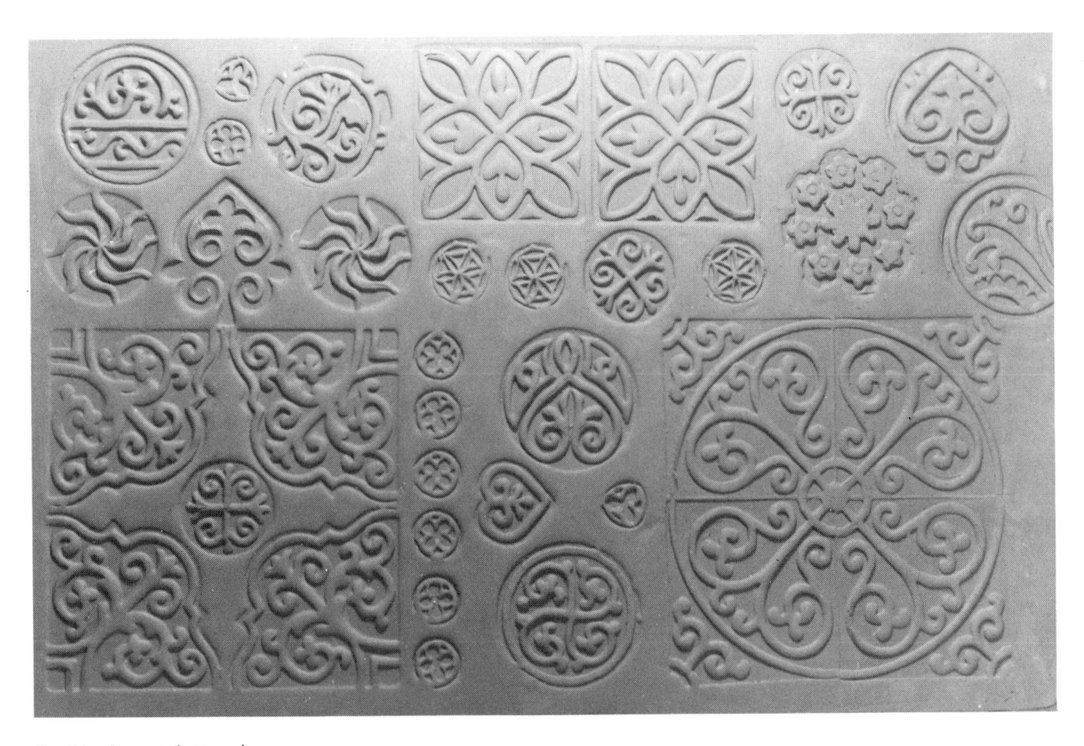

Combined stamp impressions.

Bisque mold. Persia, 10th–11th century. The Metropolitan Museum of Art, Gift of Charles B. Hoyt, 1932. Molds like this were used to form bowls or sections of bottles or jars. The decoration in many such molds was intricately carved, but this one is rather casually impressed with six small stamps.

ume of the space to be filled, and the amount of plaster is calculated from that.

Plaster has long been a useful material in the potter's studio for making bats, wedging boards, press molds, and stamps. But many potters prefer to use other materials for these purposes to avoid the danger of contaminating the clay; plaster crumbs in the clay expand in the kiln and cause little chunks of the pot to blow off. Plaster is, however, a convenient, useful, and satisfying material to employ if the necessary care is taken to avoid clay contamination. Hands, tools, and mixing bowls should be cleaned in a bucket of water immediately after working with plaster. Sediment should be disposed of in the trash, *not* down plumbing drains, as it will clog them. Rasps should be cleaned with a wire brush before plaster hardens on them. When the casting or carving operation has been completed, the area should be thoroughly cleaned to get rid of all plaster crumbs and scraps.

Earthenware bottle. Persia, 12th–13th century. The Metropolitan Museum of Art, Rogers Fund, 1912. This bottle was made in three sections, the neck and the bottom half of the body wheelthrown, the top half of the body formed in a decorated mold similar to the one shown at left.

WOOD STAMPS

Wood is one of the best materials for stamps because it is porous, yet durable, even when carved with very intricate, delicate designs. An easy way to make wood stamps is with an ordinary handsaw; a surprising variety of designs can be made with the straight, thin lines this tool imposes. More varied designs can be made with simple woodcarving tools, which are made in a number of shapes. With six or eight tools, almost any type of cut can be made, but perhaps three are enough to begin with: a V-gouge, or veiner, a U-gouge, and a flat chisel. A small electric router can be used to cut patterns on larger surfaces. With practice, elaborate designs can be made very quickly.

Softwood, such as pine, will work, but only the end grain should be used, as it is difficult to cut across the grain without causing splintering. Ends of dowels, as well as the ends of 2x4s and 4x4s, are convenient sizes. Hardwoods with close, fine, straight grain will cut more cleanly and are more durable.

These wood stamps (largest about 5" in diameter) were made by the author except where otherwise noted. Round stamps at top center and lower right are Greek bread stamps, rectangular pair (upper right) are from England (for butter or cookies). Small round ones at top are cut from dowels or spools. The others are carved in end grain of soft wood.

WOOD PADDLES

Wood paddles—used for altering thrown pots or for sealing joints and refining shapes in slab or coil construction—may be patterned so that the paddling imparts texture. A bold, simple grid pattern on a paddle may be impressed clearly on the pot by smacking it sharply. Or a subtle, complex, weblike texture may be produced by overlaying light strokes at different angles. Paddles may also be used as stamps. Wrapped with cord, twine, or coarse material such as burlap, paddles will produce distinctive textures.

It is good to have a variety of sizes and shapes of paddles. They seem to be most convenient when they are about 12″ to 16″ long, 1½″ to 4″ wide, and ⅜″ to ¾″ thick. Softwoods (pine or redwood) seem best, as they are more absorbent and less likely to stick when used on wet pots.

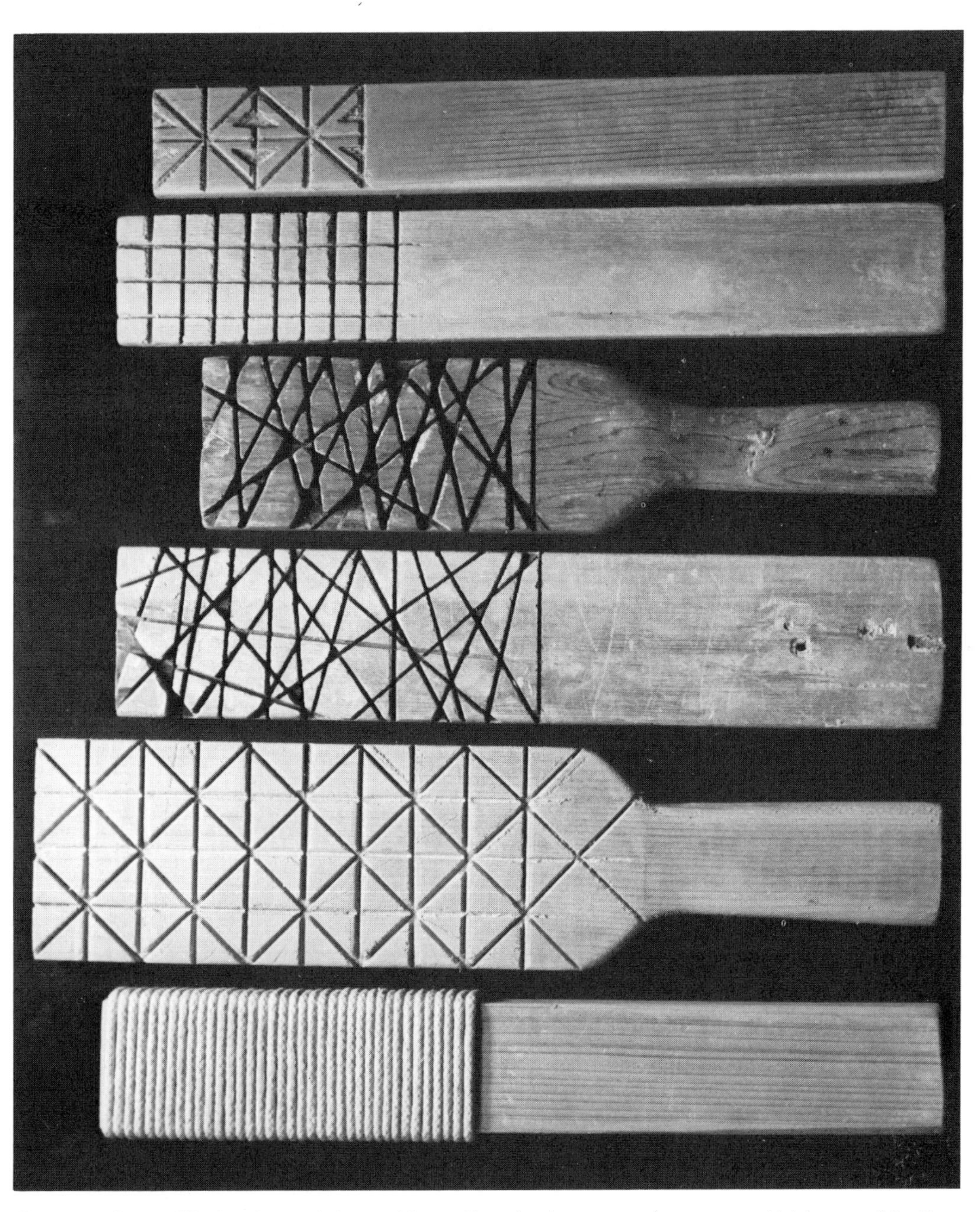

Patterns on these paddles have been entirely cut with an ordinary handsaw, except the one at top which has carved details, and one at bottom which is cord wrapped.

ROLLING STAMPS

Rolling stamps, or roulettes, are excellent for making bands of decoration, especially on thrown pieces on which it is awkward to impress a flat stamp. These may be made from wood, clay, or plaster, the pattern being made on the curved surface of a cylinder. It is easiest to make these of clay, as curved wood or plaster surfaces are awkward to work on. Plaster roulettes can be created by making a design in a rectangle of clay, then rolling this into a cylinder with the pattern inside, the hollow forming a mold which can be filled with plaster.

Roulettes are more convenient to use if provided with an axle and handle, but this is not necessary if they can be rotated easily in the hand. Designs can also be carved into furniture casters, preferably of wood, although plastic or rubber can be used.

Salt-glazed jug. England (Nottingham) 1770. Except for a few incised lines, the decoration was done with small, sharply detailed stamps and roulettes. A smooth brown salt glaze adds to a tooled-leather look.

Rolling stamps or roulettes can impress continuous linear decoration on slabs or soft pots. A handle helps to maintain even pressure as the stamp rolls but may not be necessary if there are hemispherical indentations in the flat sides, allowing the stamp to be rotated while held firmly between thumb and forefinger.

Designs can be made in clay, then cast in plaster to make stamps. The clay mold at right with decorations on wall instead of bottom will form a roulette.

CORD-IMPRESSED DECORATION

One of the most fascinating types of impressed decoration is the cord marking on the Jomon pottery of neolithic Japan. The Jomon period continued for several thousand years, ending about 300 B.C., and several distinct styles developed. The interest in cord-impressed texture continued throughout the period although it did not appear on all the pottery. The name Jomon, meaning "cord-marked," first applied to the pottery by a 19th-century scholar, became the name for the entire culture. The earliest cord markings were made by a piece of cord wrapped around the potter's thumb or finger or a strip laid on the pot and pressed. Later, short lengths of cord were rolled on the surface of the pot, creating a wealth of different patterns by being twisted, braided, or knotted in various ways. Cord-wrapped sticks produced another kind of texture, varied by spiral, double-spiral, and fish-net winding of the cord, by knotting, or by combining two or more types of cord. Cords or cord-wrapped sticks about 6″ long are convenient to use. They can be rolled on soft slabs or on the walls of pots using the palm and fingers of the hand in the same way a coil of clay is formed.

Stoneware footed compote, stamped and incised decoration, copper-red glaze, 5″ x 9½″ in diameter. James McKinnell, U.S.A.

Braided cord or rope leaves a distinct impression when rolled on soft clay.

Pilgrim bottle, Syria. Press-molded body; neck and handles added.

Urn. Japan, middle Jomon period, ca. 2000 B.C. Although only 15″ high, this piece has a monumental sculptural quality. The upper part is decorated with added elements and deep carving, while the bottom part is cord impressed.

FOUR

ADDED DECORATION

Adding separate clay elements to a pot, whether they are purely ornamental or basically functional appendages, is essentially different from other decorative techniques which involve coloring, manipulating, or cutting into the pot. Added decoration, even in low relief, usually alters the contour of the pot more than stamping or carving; and handles, spouts, or sculptural additions are in fact separate forms, which can create new composite shapes or can become a kind of counterpoint to the basic form. However, insensitively used, these additions may overwhelm or obscure the pot itself.

SPRIGGING

Sprigging is a process of adding relief decoration to a damp pot. The decorative clay elements (sprigs) have traditionally been thin press-molded appliqués, but they may also be in the form of slabs, strips, coils, dabs, shavings, or trimmings, and may be carved or stamped after being applied to the pot.

Press-molded sprigs were used in China as early as the Han dynasty (206 B.C.–220 A.D.). These took the form of narrow bands or friezes, or small masks or medallions, used singly, in pairs as subtle accents, or as part of stylized lugs or handles. Tradition confined the sprigs to a few types used in specific ways.

During the T'ang dynasty (618–906 A.D.), decoration of all types became more lavish and colorful, and sprigging was used more freely. The most common sprigs were stylized floral rosettes or medallions and leafy scrolls, used individually and in groups. Some pots were embellished with only one or two sprigs, while others were almost completely covered with a profusion of smaller relief bosses.

Exceptionally varied and elaborate use of sprigged decoration can be seen on various types of pottery made in Germany in the 16th century. One of the best known standard forms is the bellarmine or *Bartmannkrug*, a round-bellied jug on the neck of which is a press-molded face with a flowing beard. The jugs are usually further enriched with medallions, rosettes, scrolls, or coats of arms. Many cylindrical forms or the cylindrical portions of more complex forms are decorated with large, intricately detailed sprig panels or friezes. These wrap around the pots, depicting biblical, mythological, or genre scenes, often copied from contemporary woodcuts or engravings. Some pots are decorated with tiny coils laid on in vinelike patterns, enriched with press-molded sprigs of individual leaves of acanthus or oak, sometimes with acorns. On others the coils are used to define bands or arcades framing press-molded figures. Most of these wares were salt glazed, unifying form and decoration, while enhancing the sprigs.

Bowl with alligator lid, 16" high. Costa Rica (Pre-Columbian, after A.D. 1000), Guanacaste Province, Filadelfia. Yale University Art Gallery. Perhaps the grotesque, yet delightful stylized alligator cannot really be considered decoration at all, but a small sculpture mounted on top of a lidded jar. It is indeed the dominant and most interesting part of the piece.

Applying Sprigs. Sprigged decoration can be done on damp thrown or handbuilt pots (stiff enough to be handled, but preferably softer than leatherhard) or on slabs before they are assembled. The area to be decorated is coated with slip (usually made from the same clay as the pot). In applying strips, coils, or slabs, each piece can be firmly pressed as it is applied or the entire pattern can be laid in place, then lightly paddled to adhere it to the slipped surface. Intricate patterns can be made using narrow strips cut from a thin slab, but small coils are more flexible and therefore much better for floral designs. Guidelines for complex decoration can be sketched in the soft clay of the pot or slab before the slip is applied. After all the strips or coils are in place, light paddling will give a uniform surface as well as good adhesion.

The sprigs should normally be about the same consistency as, or a little softer than, the pot or slab to which they are applied. However, an interesting inlaid appearance can be achieved by using sprigs slightly stiffer than the background and paddling them until they are flush with the surface, while retaining their outline. The same effect can be achieved by laying out the sprig design on a board or plaster bat, then placing a somewhat softer slab over it and rolling with a rolling pin. The sprig design should be lightly brushed with slip before the slab is laid over it. Another variation is to develop the design on a hump mold or in a press mold and then press the clay over it.

Molded sprigs cannot, of course, be paddled or firmly pressed to seal them to the pot without damaging their designs. The sprig can, however, be carefully lifted out of the mold and gently pressed into place. Or, while the sprig is still in the mold, the slipped surface of the pot, supported from inside with the other hand, can be firmly pressed against the mold. The sprig will adhere to the pot and easily release from its mold, provided the clay is not sticky and the mold is not wet. The technique is very easy for small stamps on any surface, or for larger ones on flat surfaces, but becomes more difficult with large sprigs on curved surfaces. A similar effect can be obtained by first applying slabs, dabs, or strips of soft clay to the pot, then pressing stamps into them. For further discussion of stamps see Chapter 3.

Two mugs, Henry Lyman, U.S.A. Slab-built of low-fire white clay, the mugs are decorated with small coils and slabs of clay. The one on the left has been first impressed with a crocheted pattern.

Les Miley gently presses strips and dabs of clay onto the slip-coated surface of the leatherhard pot.

After all of the sprigs are in place, light paddling insures good adhesion and evens the surface.

The sprigs are embellished with incising and impressing.

Stoneware plate with sprigged decoration, Les Miley, U.S.A. The glaze was sponged off the raised portions of the design but remains in the depressions.

A small extruder (this one from Kemper, about 4" long) quickly makes perfect tiny coils, ideal for sprigged decoration.

Porcelain covered jar and footed bowl, about 4" high. Wilhelm and Elly Kuch, Germany, 1974. The decoration of tiny coils and dabs was laid out in hemispherical plaster press molds; clay was then pressed into the decoration so that the surface is somewhat like that of an incised decoration, but with a distinctly different character. The decoration is accentuated by a clear celadon glaze.

Color in Sprigged Decoration. Sprigs may be of a different color from the background, as on the decorative Jasper wares of Wedgwood, which employ white sprigs on a blue, lilac, pink, green, yellow, or black stained body. On more elaborate pieces, two colors of sprigs were used. The technical perfection of this minutely detailed decoration is amazing; the delicate sprigs are almost paper-thin in places, so that the background color glows through. Impressive in technique and workmanship, the sprigs are unfortunately cold and stiff, especially on the larger, more elaborate pieces. The smaller, less pretentious ones are more appealing, their jewellike precision seeming more appropriate to their scale. When this ware was first made in 1775, the body was stained before forming, but later the stain was applied to the surface before adding the decoration.

Sprigs can be made of a different-colored clay from that used to make the pot, provided the shrinkage rate is similar. The slip used for attaching the sprigs may be of a contrasting color also, but this requires careful work and a minimum of handling to avoid smudging.

Another way of emphasizing the decoration is to glaze the pot while leaving the sprigs unglazed. This can achieve an effective contrast, but in some cases it makes the decoration appear superficial and poorly integrated. Therefore, whether a dramatic contrast or the unifying effect of an overall color and texture is better must be decided in each case.

*Salt-glazed stoneware jug (*Bartmannkrug*), Germany (Cologne), late 16th century. Fitzwilliam Museum, Cambridge. The face and beard are sprigs; the stars are made with round medallions surrounded by separate triangular sprigs, the same triangle forms used around the neck.*

Amphora with dragon-head handles. China, T'ang dynasty, Chicago Art Institute. Although a conventionalized design, there is considerable variety in the details of the dragon handles which always have a lively individual quality.

HANDLES

Handles have been an important part of many pottery shapes for several thousand years. They have sometimes been treated as purely functional appendages, simply made and quickly attached in the most convenient place, or blended as unobtrusively as possible with the form. But more often their decorative possibilities have been exploited, even to the detriment of their function, and many otherwise unremarkable pots have been enlivened or ruined by fanciful handles. Handles have been molded, carved, elongated, twisted, contorted, and exaggerated, sometimes becoming the dominant element of a pot.

Some unusual handles have been the inspiration of individual potters, while others are the result, through years of repetition, of a gradual evolutionary development. Originally functional handles metamorphosed into purely decorative forms, either through diminution or exaggeration, and similar processes in reverse made handles of decorative motifs. Many fanciful handles are the result of embellishment or manipulation of simple pulled or thrown handles or knobs, while the most bizarre and fantastic ones are actually small, molded, constructed, or carved sculptures—decoration which functions as handles, rather than decorated handles.

There are many examples of animal forms or animal heads used as handles. In Chinese ceramics, small handles or lugs appear in the shape of elephant heads, fish, or dragons, realistically modeled, stylized, or even transformed into curious arabesques. My own favorites are the dragon-headed handles on T'ang dynasty amphorae. Although conventional in form, each one has a lively, individual quality. Braided or twisted handles, perhaps originally inspired by those on woven baskets, have appeared in many versions, some fanciful, charming, even graceful, others funny or grotesque. English potters in the 17th and 18th centuries made some wonderfully outlandish pots by festooning some of their normal forms with exuberantly exaggerated handles, knobs, and other applied decoration.

Of the many types of handles discussed above, some were made by carving or molding, while others were assembled from small coils, dabs, or slabs, with details sometimes added by carving, incising, piercing, or molding.

Porcelain covered jar, 16″ high. Jonathan Kaplan, U.S.A.. The form is elegant, yet unconventional in its proportions, and the whimsical, yet graceful handles are a delightful complement to the form, in spite of the tenuous nature of their relationship.

The Robert Brent hand extruder is heavily constructed and can hold 10 pounds of clay. Dies can easily be made from metal, plastic, masonite, or clay.

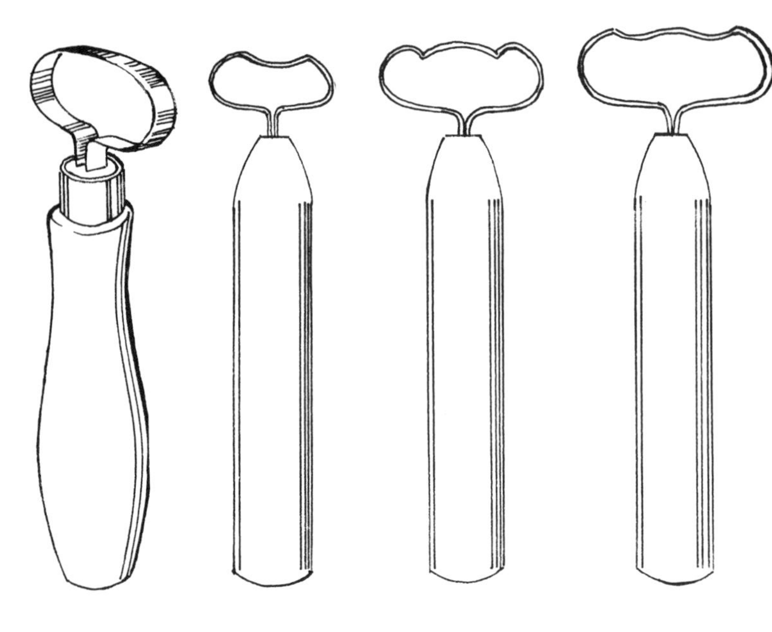

Handle cutters

Tools for Making Handles. Most contemporary potters make traditional pulled handles, and certainly no other method can quite duplicate the flowing, organic quality of a well-pulled handle. There are, however, three ways of making strap handles similar in appearance to pulled ones, but easier and quicker to make. These techniques also have the potential for making handles quite different from pulled ones.

The first method is to roll or extrude a coil of fairly soft clay, slightly flatten it by pressing gently along the length of it with the thumb, so that it has an oval shape, then smooth it with a wet sponge or chamois held tightly around the fingers. This must be done with only a few light, firm strokes or the coil will be completely flattened. The cross-section can appear simply as a slightly flattened oval or it can have one or more grooves or ridges, depending on how the sponge or chamois is held. More complex cross-sections can be developed using a profile rib or template of wood or plastic similar to those discussed in Chapter 2 under Convex Fluting and Templates.

The other two methods are mechanical and have the advantages of speed, uniformity, and precision, but the disadvantage of requiring a separate tool or die for each variation in handle size or shape.

Wire handle cutters, simply a variation on the ubiquitous wire loop modeling or trimming tool, are available commercially or can easily be made in any desired shape or size from stiff wire. The homemade tool can be fitted with a wooden handle, or the ends of the wire may simply be twisted together. To cut a handle, the loop end of the tool is simply pulled through a well-wedged block of soft clay.

A large extruder, such as those made by Robert Brent Corporation or Scott Creek Pottery, is ideal for making large numbers of identical handles. Blank dies can be cut to any desired handle cross-section. Dies can be cut from steel, aluminum, plastic, Masonite, or clay. Clay dies are quickest and easiest to make but must be fired to maturity before using. Blank steel dies are available for both extruders, and although it is more difficult to cut than the other materials, steel is the most durable and is best for complex or finely detailed extrusions. Even hollow handles can be made with these tools. To operate the extruder, the cylinder is simply filled with soft clay and the plunger is pushed to force the clay through the die, extruding perfect strips or tubes.

Earthenware posset pot England (Bristol), early 18th century. The Metropolitan Museum of Art, Gift of R. Thornton Wilson, 1937. Posset was a mixture of hot ale, wine or other liquor, milk, sugar, and spices sometimes thickened with bread or cake, and often drunk from the spout of a posset pot. The form was common in 18th-century England, made with many variations in decoration, from quite simple to ridiculously elaborate. This delightful example has majolica decoration in blue, as well as fancifully constructed handles.

SPOUTS

Spouts, like handles, have decorative possibilities overlooked by most contemporary potters. The simple, unassuming wheelthrown spout is often the most appropriate, but some forms may accept or even demand something different. John Glick has explored the possibilities of bold S-curved spouts which would fit more naturally with his slab-built teapots. He has constructed square-section spouts with slabs and has made hexagonal spouts using a two-piece plaster press mold.

To make such a mold, a solid clay model is made, sliced in half when almost leatherhard, then laid cut-face down on a smooth, slick surface, such as Formica or glass, and surrounded by mold frames made of clay, wood, or linoleum sealed with clay. Plaster is poured into the forms to cover the models about 1″ to 2″ When set, the mold frames and clay models are removed, any burrs or sharp edges are smoothed, and the mold, after a few hours of drying, is ready to use.

A simple press mold does not need the ball-and-socket keys used on slip molds to insure accurate alignment, but if desired they can be made by the following process. Half of the mold is formed as above. When it has set, two or more shallow sockets (hemispherical depressions about ½″ in diameter) are carved into the fresh plaster, which is then coated with mold soap. Both halves of the model are put in place, a new retaining wall made, and the second half of the mold poured onto the first.

To make the spout, a thin slab of clay is pressed into each half, then trimmed. The edges are coated with slip, the two halves joined together, then removed from the mold, and the joint trimmed and smoothed. Handles can also be made in this way. (For more information on using plaster, see Chapter 3.)

In the past, spouts have taken some strange forms, appearing in China often in the shape of bird or dragon heads. An interesting form which has appeared in many versions in different locations is a round-bodied ewer with long neck and very long spout springing from the body and joined to the neck with a small bracket or brace. Originally a medieval Persian metal shape, it was copied in clay, not only in the Middle East but in China and Korea as well, and appears again in a rather stiff form as the *Schnabelkanne* in 16th-century Germany. In all these variations, the long, thin-bracketed spout—straight or curved, plain or lavishly decorated with brushwork, carving, or sprigs—is the dominant feature.

Attachment of Handles and Spouts. The place where the handle or spout is to be attached should be scratched and slipped; the handle or spout should be slightly softer than the pot. As the appendage will tend to dry more quickly than the body of the pot, the piece should be dried slowly.

Spouts, handles, and lugs, however flamboyant or subtle, must be carefully considered both in size and shape in relation to the pot and in their placement on the pot. The most perfect spout or handle, if placed too high or too low, can throw off the balance of the piece; even small lugs must be carefully placed on the curve of the shoulder in a comfortable relation to the neck or rim. The attachment itself can be very important. Often the quickest and simplest way is most satisfactory, but some articulation or elaboration can be very effective when done decisively. A fussy, overworked attachment is a sure sign of inept craftsmanship.

Stoneware ewer, 9″ high. China, T'ang dynasty. Cleveland Museum of Art. Press-molded sprigs, triple-coil handles, and a faceted spout enliven the simple, solid form, while remaining clearly subordinate to it.

*(Left) Salt-glazed stoneware ewer (*Schnabelkanne*), Germany (Siegburg), 16th century. Even the spout is decorated with sprigged panels.*

Porcelain ewer. China, Ting Ware, 12th–13th century. Fitzwilliam Museum, Cambridge. The form is simple and clean, the spout small and discreet, and the elaborately detailed handle with its triple-press-molded attachments adds a lively, fanciful touch without spoiling the basic serenity of the pot.

ACCENTUATION OF SCULPTURAL DECORATION

Sculptural decoration, whether resulting from the forming process or deliberately carved, impressed, or added, may be effectively accented or enhanced through glaze or stain treatments. In some cases it may be desirable to play down the three-dimensional decoration by application of an opaque glaze. Often, however, the decoration is made most effective by using color to accent it.

All the methods discussed below involve applications of color or glaze, which are altered by the sculptural surface itself during firing. Sculptural decoration can also be enhanced by using glazes, slips, or colorants to fill in shapes outlined by incising, added elements, or impressed designs, the sculptural decoration serving as a framework for color application.

GLAZES

Sculptural decoration can be very subtly accented by a glaze which flows a little in the firing, causing it to be thinner on edges and thicker in depressions. The appearance of any glaze is affected by its thickness, and some change dramatically with slight variations in thickness. The shallow, delicate, carved decoration of Chinese Sung dynasty porcelains is often accented by a pale, transparent celadon glaze which fires darker where it pools in the incisions. The carving is given dramatic emphasis, but the effect is so perfect and natural that it seems an integral part of the pot.

The celadon colors are produced by the presence of iron oxide in the glaze in reduction firing. From .5% to 2% red iron oxide produces gray to gray-green, while higher percentages, up to 3% or 4%, produce light to dark olive green. The iron in old Chinese glazes was probably added in the form of red clay or ochre. For effective accentuation of sculptural decoration, the glaze should be transparent or semitransparent and works best over a light-colored body. Iron in the body darkens the glaze color, and a dark body obscures color variation in the glaze. Celadons are usually thought of as high-temperature glazes (cone 6 to 10), but similar colors can be produced at much lower temperatures.

Reduction glazes which contain a very high percentage of iron (8% to 10%) may fire smooth black where thick and red-brown where thin on edges. As accentuation of sculptural decoration, these saturated-iron glazes tend to be irregular, fuzzy, and somewhat unpredictable, but the effects can be very rich and spectacular.

Copper-red glazes developed in reduction firing may vary from green-tinged beige to intense pink-red on the same pot depending on thickness and firing conditions. This color variation sometimes accents sculptural deco-

Roman amphora, 100 B.C.–300 A.D., said to have come from Syria. The Metroplitan Museum of Art, Gift of John D. Rockfeller, 1938. The fluid blue glaze is darker where it pools in depressions, accenting the carved, stamped, and sprigged decoration.

Porcelain dish, 7" in diameter. China, Sung dynasty. British Museum. Every nuance of the exquisitely carved decoration is perfectly revealed and accented by the pale-gray transparent celadon glaze.

Water pot, 5" in diameter. China, K'ang-hsi (1622–1722). University of London, Percival David Foundation of Chinese Art. The delicately incised decoration is accented by a copper-red glaze. Glazes of this type are erratic in color development, and the decoration on many similar pieces has been obscured rather than accented by the glaze.

Ewer. China. Freer Gallery of Art. A matt-black glaze which breaks to reddish brown on edges brings out details of handle, lugs, and spout.

Vase. Stig Lyndberg, Sweden. The sprigged and impressed decoration is beautifully enhanced by a copper-red glaze, although the color variations do not faithfully follow the relief surface.

ration in dramatically beautiful ways, but it is unpredictable and difficult to control.

The color of opaque matt glazes changes with thickness, especially when a light-colored glaze is used over a dark body. Very beautiful, soft, fuzzy effects may be achieved with these glazes, but fine detail is lost.

Carved, stamped, or added decoration can be accented by partial removal of a glaze coating. The still-wet glaze can be wiped or scraped off the high parts of the decoration, leaving it undisturbed in the depressions. Essentially the same result can be achieved by coating the raised decoration with wax resist, so that the glaze does not adhere to it (see Chapter 6 for more on wax resist). A more subtle contrast can be achieved by rubbing a dry, powdery glaze coating with the hand or a piece of abrasive screen, thereby thinning but not removing the glaze from the raised parts of the form.

Dish. China, 14th century, University of London, Percival David Foundation of Chinese Art. The unglazed sprigged decoration is isolated against a cool, jadelike celadon glaze.

OXIDE STAINS AND SLIPS

The natural surface of the clay can be retained while boldly accenting sculptural decoration through the use of an oxide solution. This stains the surface of the bisqued pot instead of forming a coating over it, to bring out every nuance of design or texture without imposing a texture or surface quality of its own.

In practice, the coloring oxide is mixed with water, for example, for iron oxide about 2 teaspoons for each cup of water, to make a wash which is sponged or brushed onto the bisqued pot, completely covering the area to be stained. The surface is then wiped with a wet sponge, removing most of the oxide from the high parts of the form, while leaving deposits in the depressions. Then the area is wiped with a clean, wet sponge. If the wiping is done lightly, even the shallowest line or texture will hold some oxide. Sharply defined raised decoration can be accented by lightly brushing the surface with a flat sponge or brush charged with oxide, so that only the raised portions are stained while the depressions are passed over.

The most commonly used colorant is iron oxide, which produces in reduction firing a color range from light red-brown to metallic black. Manganese dioxide gives a similar, but grayer, less lively color. Strong color contrast can be achieved only on a light-colored body, but light-colored stain or slip can be used in a similar way to contrast with a dark body. Red iron oxide, manganese dioxide, rutile (warm tan yellow), and tin-vanadium stain (yellow) can be used as stains mixed only with water, but most colorants need to be mixed in a slip or covered by a glaze to produce their colors.

A glaze can be applied over slip- or oxide-accented sculptural decoration with the colored pattern showing through clearly or indistinctly, depending on the nature and thickness of the glaze. Shallow carved or stamped decoration which might be lost under a thick, opaque glaze can be defined in this way.

Partial glazing with contrasting areas of oxide-treated carved or impressed decoration against smooth glazed areas can intensify the character of both.

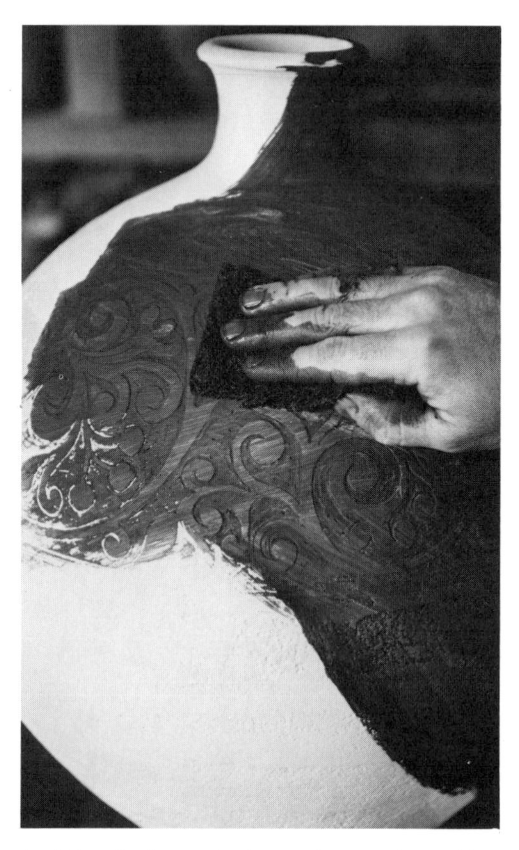

A solution of red iron oxide in water is sponged onto a bisque-fired pot.

The pot is wiped with a clean, wet sponge to remove most of the oxide coating from raised areas, leaving deposits in the depressions.

Earthenware covered jar. Guatemala, Mayan. Museum of the American Indian, Heye Foundation. The burnished clay is a dark red-brown to black, contrasting strongly with the white slip rubbed into the incisions of the carved decoration.

Slab-built stoneware bottle, 10" high, by the author, 1974. The decoration was impressed with a plaster stamp, then stained with iron oxide after bisque firing.

SALT GLAZE

Salt glazing accents sculptural decoration in a wonderfully rich and subtle way. The glaze itself is thin and transparent and tends to pool in depressions, emphasing rather than concealing even the finest details.

The process of salt glazing was developed in the late 14th or early 15th century by German stoneware potters in the Rhineland. At about the same time they began to embellish their simple forms with intricately detailed sprigged decoration which was beautifully enhanced by the salt glaze (see Chapter 4 for more information on sprigging).

Salt glaze is a natural vapor glaze formed on the ware during firing. When the firing approaches the maturing temperature of the clay, ordinary coarse salt is introduced into the kiln, where it immediately vaporizes into sodium and chlorine, filling the kiln with dense clouds of vapor. The sodium reacts with silica in the clay to form a thin glaze. When the cloudy kiln atmosphere begins to clear, more salt is added. This process is repeated until the desired glaze thickness has formed on the ware, as indicated by draw trials of the same clay. These small rings are lined up behind a spy hole and pulled out at intervals during the salting to check the progress of the glaze formation. Because of the circulation patterns of the salt vapor among the pots, some of a kiln load and even parts of the same pot are inevitably more thickly glazed than others, but unpredictable variations are often a part of the beauty of salt-glazed pots.

The color of salt glaze (ranging from white, cream, gray, or tan to various shades of

Plate. Germany (Crefeld), 1739. Victoria and Albert Museum. Colored lead glazes have been used in various periods and cultures to fill in incised or impressed linear designs, notably in T'ang dynasty China, the Islamic Middle East, and 18th-century Germany and Eastern Europe. The delightfully naïve incised decoration shown here is embellished with yellow, brown, and green lead glazes applied within the framework of the incised lines.

*Salt-glazed jug (*Bartmannkrug*). Germany, mid 16th century, Cologne or Frechen. Victoria and Albert Museum. Every detail of the elaborate sprigged decoration is faithfully picked out by the salt glaze.*

brown) depends on the clay body and the thickness of the salt accumulation, and the amount of reduction in the kiln. The glaze can be fairly smooth in texture and color, but it is normally pebbly and often mottled in color. On very dark bodies the salt may be an uninteresting dark brown, while on white clay it can be rather bland.

The natural color range can be varied by decorating with slips or oxides—iron, cobalt, manganese, and rutile being the colorants used most often. Decoration with white slip on a medium or dark body is also very effective. Ware to be salted need not be bisque fired, so decoration is done on wet or leatherhard pots. The salt vapor does not reach interior surfaces of closed or constricted forms, and if these are to be glazed, a normal glaze must be applied.

Salt glazing has usually been associated with stoneware and is most often done in the cone 5 to cone 10 range, although it can be done successfully as low as cone 04 as long as the clay used matures at the firing temperature.

A downdraft kiln is best for salt firing, as it forces a longer circulation of the salt vapors among the pots. The interior walls must be of hard brick or high-alumina castable refractory. The kiln can be fired with wood, oil, or gas. There are several disadvantages in salt firing besides its unpredictability. The interior of a kiln used for salt firing becomes itself salt glazed, making it unsuitable for normal glaze firing. The salt vapor has a corrosive effect on the kiln, so that more frequent repairs are necessary. The buildup of salt glaze on kiln walls and furniture can be retarded, but not prevented, by coating the shelves and supports with aluminum-oxide slip.

One of the most serious problems is the toxic chlorine vapor emitted from the kiln during firing. The kiln must be in a well-ventilated area, preferably outdoors, to protect the operator. This does not, however, solve the problem of the billowing clouds issuing from the stack, which may be objectionable in populated areas. In the 16th century, the potters were forced out of Cologne, one of the early salt-glaze centers in Germany, largely because of the excessive air pollution. Recently, successful experiments have been conducted substituting sodium carbonate (soda ash) or sodium bicarbonate (baking soda) for all or part of the salt, thus eliminating or reducing the chlorine fumes.

Salt-glazed stoneware teapot with slip-trailed decoration. Don Pilcher, U.S.A. Collection of Ken Deavers.

Porcelain bowl. China, Yüan dynasty. Freer Gallery of Art. The very precise brushwork is done in several shades of cobalt blue under a clear glaze.

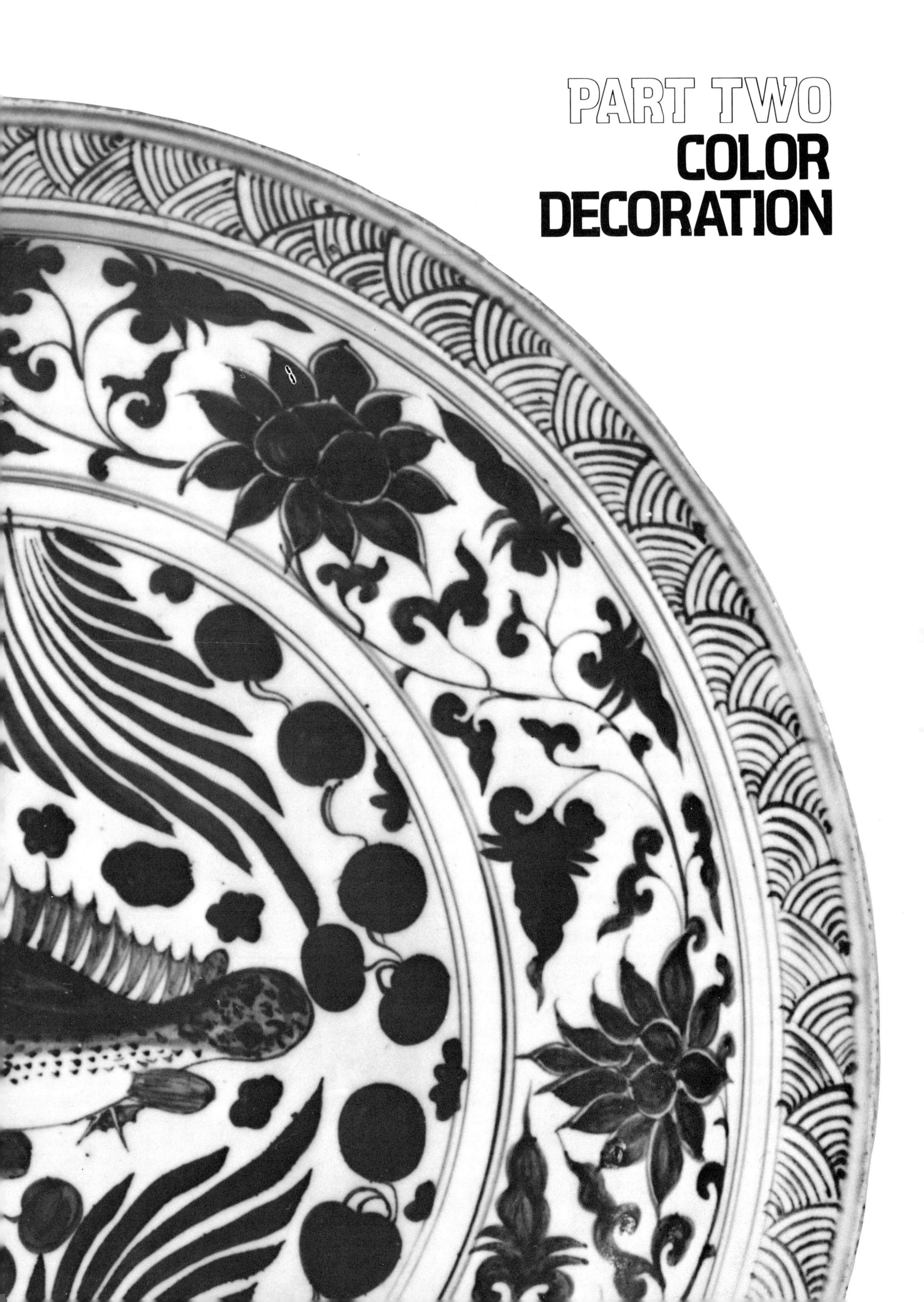

PART TWO
COLOR DECORATION

SLIPS, UNDERGLAZE AND MAJOLICA

Although most of the basic techniques for using colored slips, oxide solutions, or underglaze pigments have been used by potters for hundreds or even thousands of years, some are comparatively new. Moreover, there are countless variations and combinations which, along with modern, refined raw materials and colorants, provide a wide range of possibilities. Some techniques are done on wet or leather-hard pots, some on bisque ware, and some over a raw glaze coating, while others may be used at all three stages.

SLIPS AND ENGOBES

Painting with colored clay slips is one of the oldest and most widespread forms of pottery decoration. Colored slips were used in many different cultures long before the discovery of glazes, and slip-decorated pottery 6,000 to 7,000 years old has been found at numerous sites in the Middle East. During the 5th millennium B.C., sophisticated decorative styles were developed in Mesopotamia, Persia, and Egypt, most often employing red decoration directly on the pot or over a white or cream slip coating. The Tel Halaf culture of Iraq produced pieces with quite elaborate polychrome decoration in red, white, and black slips on a buff body.

Vigorous and dynamic slip-decorated pieces were made by Minoan potters on the island of Crete between 2000 and 1400 B.C. The best of these show a wonderful relation between form and decoration—the curvilinear and spiral designs very bold and self-assertive, yet perfectly enveloping and enhancing the full, round forms.

The Greeks, the Iberians, the Chinese, and the Indians of the Americas also produced beautiful, elaborately decorated pottery using only the limited palette of natural clay slips; and indeed the beauty and dignity of much of this early work is directly related to the limited color and textural range.

Later the coloring of white slips with metallic oxides to produce a wider range of color, and the use of clear or colored glazes over them, along with new techniques of application, greatly increased possibilities of slip decoration.

Slip may be used simply to color part of a pot by dipping, brushing, pouring, or spraying, or this coating may be partially removed as in sgraffito or mishima. The slip can be applied in patterns with a brush or slip trailer; it can be used with wax resist or stencils; or it can be printed with a silkscreen.

The terms engobe and slip are often used interchangeably, and technically there is little difference. Engobe usually refers to a slip coating over an entire surface to mask the body color or to serve as a background for decora-

Panathenaic amphora. Greek (Attic), ca. 530–520 B.C. The Metropolitan Museum of Art, Fletcher Fund, 1956. One of the vases which were filled with oil and awarded to the victors in the Panathenaic games. The decoration, painted in black slip on a red body, with details in sgraffito, depicts the goddess Athena on one side and the event for which the prize was given on the other.

Earthenware jar. China, Neolithic period. Freer Gallery of Art. The exceptionally bold decoration in red and black slips on a buff body gives this small jar a monumental quality.

tion or to a slip composed predominantly of nonclay materials.

Slip Composition. Slip decorating is usually done on pots when they are wet to leather-hard, but it may also be done on dry or bisque ware if an appropriate slip formula is used. For application on wet pots, a slip made from the clay body itself works well; and if the clay color is light, a good color range is possible by the addition of various oxides. If a dark body is used, it is preferable to start with a slip based on china clay, ball clay, and feldspar, or nepheline syenite and flint, which can be used as a white slip or as a neutral base for adding colorants.

For use on wet pots, the slip composition is normally about half or more raw clay. During drying, the pot and its slip coating shrink together, but for use on dry or bisque pots, such a slip would tend to crack and fall off as it dried, because there would be no accompanying shrinkage in the pot. To reduce shrinkage in the slip, some of the raw clay is replaced with calcined clay and the feldspar or nepheline syenite increased. The raw clay in the slip may be about 30% to 40% for dry pots and only 20% to 25% for bisque. (Suggested slip compositions and colorants are given in the Appendix.)

Slips have a much wider firing range than most glazes, and proportions of the ingredients may vary considerably with essentially the same results. Most slip formulas for any temperature range include 5% borax, which forms a tougher dry coat (especially important when glaze is to be applied over a raw slip), and 5% zircopax for opacity.

Natural slips, such as Barnard and Albany (both dark brown when fired), can be used on wet or damp clay or on bisque ware (in a thin solution) to accent impressed, carved, or added decoration. When fired to stoneware temperatures they will form a buttery matt glaze.

Very thick slip coatings, and especially techniques such as slip trailing, feather combing, and marbling (discussed later in this chapter), can be done safely only on wet-to-damp pots and must be dried very slowly to prevent rapid shrinkage and consequent cracking and flaking.

Spouted jug. Iran, 1100–1000 B.C. The Metropolitan Museum of Art, Gift of the Teheran Museum. The decoration, painted in red slip on a buff ground, emphasizes the elongated beaklike spout. The piece was probably intended for ritual rather than household use.

(Left) Dipylon Krater, Greek (Attic Geometric), 8th century B.C. *The Metropolitan Museum of Art, Rogers Fund, 1914. This colossal vase, almost 3½ feet high, was made as a grave monument. The slip decoration represents funeral scenes.*

Stirrup jug, 10″ high. Greek-Mycenean, 1200–1125 B.C. *The Metropolitan Museum of Art, Louisa Eldridge McBurney Gift Fund. The exuberant decoration in red and brown slips shows a strong Minoan influence. Stylized octopi embrace the full form, with casually placed fish and rosettes used as fillers.*

Jug. Turkey (Iznik), about 1570–80 B.C.Iznik, about 1570–80 A.D. Victoria and Albert Museum. The lavish decoration, carefully planned yet spirited in execution, was outlined in thin black lines on the white slip ground, then filled in with red (center band) and green (top and bottom) with calligraphic details added in blue. Covered by a transparent glaze, the colors are brilliant, but not garish.

UNDERGLAZE PIGMENTS

Underglaze painting under a transparent or semiopaque glaze has been used in many cultures to produce widely varied results. Some of the most beautiful examples are the Chinese blue-and-white porcelains of the Ming dynasty (1368–1643 A.D.), which are decorated with cobalt and covered with a transparent glaze. The clean, precise, intricately detailed patterns are often outlined in a deep indigo and filled in with varying shades of paler blue washes. The cool, austere, yet sumptuous beauty of this Chinese work imspired imitations in both color and style in Japan, the Middle East, and Europe. Perhaps the most lavish underglaze decoration is found on Turkish Iznik ware made in the late 16th and early 17th centuries. Graceful, stylized floral designs were applied in black, blue, turquoise, green, and a rich iron red over a white-slip ground, and covered with a bright, clear glaze.

The metallic oxides, such as those of iron, cobalt, copper, chrome, manganese, and titanium (rutile), used for coloring slips, can be used for underglaze decoration simply by mixing them with water. A wider range of colors and greater stability in firing are provided by commercial underglaze colors. These are mixtures of metallic coloring oxides, fluxes, and refractory materials calcined, then ground to a fine powder. Hundreds of underglaze pigments are available from various manufacturers. A complete palette is available for low-temperature work, but the color range narrows with increased temperatures. Some colorants change and others disappear at stoneware temperatures. Reduction firing also changes many colors and prevents the development of others.

Application of Underglaze Pigments. Commercial underglaze colors are available in powder form and can be used on unfired pots with only water as a medium. For painting on bisque ware, small amounts are normally mixed with water and a few drops of glycerine to the consistency of smoothly flowing paint. The intensity of color obtained from commercial underglaze colors or oxide solutions depends on the thickness of application, and various shades are possible depending on the amount of water used to thin the colorant.

If applied too thickly, colorants may cause crawling or blistering of the covering glaze or make it wrinkled and metallic. If too thin, the color will be pale or even completely disappear. The proper thickness varies with the particular oxide or stain and the type and thickness of the covering glaze. Underglaze color is usually applied with a brush, but it may also be sprayed, poured, dipped, or printed.

When applied on bisque ware, a small amount of dextrin, gum arabic, or acrylic medium can be added to the colorant to produce a tougher dry coat. The decoration can also be sprayed with a thin film of gum arabic, so that the pattern will not be damaged when the glaze is applied. When the decoration is done on greenware, there is no need for a binder as the colors will harden on in the bisque firing.

Some companies sell powdered colors with a binder already added, and numerous brands are available in liquid, ready-to-use form which can be thinned with water.

In Japan, powdered cobalt has traditionally been ground with a green-tea solution which has been boiled and allowed to set to a thin, syrupy consistency. This makes a good brushing consistency and prevents smearing of the decoration when glaze is applied over it.

The burning of an organic binder in the firing may cause blistering of the glaze over the decoration, but this is unlikely unless an excessive amount of binder is used or the firing is very fast. However, if an oil medium is used, a burn-out firing to red heat is required before glazing.

Bowl, 15½" in diameter. Transoxania or Eastern Iran, Afrasiyab Ware, 10th century. Freer Gallery of Art. The sharp, clear formal decoration is painted in brownish black and brick-red slips on a white-slip ground. The stately calligraphic inscription around the rim is a proverb: "He who is content with his own opinion runs into danger," and a very common formula in Islamic pottery: "Blessing to the owner."

*Drug jar (*albarello*). Spain (Manises), middle of 15th century. Victoria and Albert Museum. The free, lyrical brush decoration flows beautifully with the shape of the jar. Some details are added in sgraffito.*

MAJOLICA

Majolica refers specifically to earthenware pottery with decoration in colored glazes or frits over an opaque white tin-lead glaze and is most often associated with Italian Renaissance and Baroque pottery. In a general sense, any decoration of metallic oxides, fritted colorants, or colored glazes applied over a raw glaze surface and fusing with the glaze in the firing could be called a majolica technique, even though the clay, glazes, firing, and appearance of the finished products might be quite different. Majolica is sometimes called on-glaze decoration because it is applied over a raw glaze, and sometimes in-glaze decoration because it fuses with the glaze in firing.

The majolica technique developed in Mesopotamia as a result of attempts to imitate the whiteness of T'ang dynasty Chinese porcelain. At first, the dark clay was hidden by a coating of white slip which served as a ground for decoration under a transparent lead glaze. In the 9th or early 10th century it was discovered that tin oxide used in a lead glaze could render it white and opaque when applied thickly, producing a smooth, bright, but not glassy surface. Decoration under or over the raw glaze fused with the glaze instead of being seen through it. Gradually the technique, along with that of metallic luster, spread throughout the Muslim world. In Spain, the mixture of Islamic and Gothic styles became what is known as Hispano-Moresque, a beautiful and unique fusion of Middle Eastern and European qualities and ideas. The calligraphic brush decoration is strong, dynamic, bold, and quickly executed, yet delicate, graceful, and carefully detailed. The forms are often stolid; the decoration, with a vigorous life of its own, sometimes ignores the form, but it has an excitement and exotic beauty unequalled in European ceramics.

The Spanish pottery was very popular among the nobility and was shipped all over Western Europe in the 14th and 15th centuries. Probably because it was often shipped from Valencia to Italy in Mallorcan vessels and perhaps by way of the island of Mallorca (Majorca), the Spanish ware became known in Italy as majorica or maiolica.

Decorated, tin-glazed pottery was already common in Italy in the 14th century, but the more sophisticated and sumptuous Spanish ware was a strong influence until the new ideas of Renaissance painting began to be applied to pottery decoration in the second half

Majolica oak-leaf drug jar. Italy (Florence), first half of 15th century. Fitzwilliam Museum. The decoration is in thickly applied cobalt blue with linear outlines in manganese brown on a white-tin glaze. The oak-leaf motif was used on a whole series of similar jars sometimes alone, more often with birds, animals, or human figures.

of the 15th century. The new Italian style, with its bright and varied palette of blue, purple, yellow, orange, brown, and green, spread across Europe. In France, tin-glazed ware was called faience, after the Italian pottery center of Faenza, and the Dutch pottery town of Delft also gave its name to the majolica technique.

On much of the Hispano-Moresque tin-glazed ware, the decoration may actually have been applied before glazing. Strong colorants, such as cobalt, can penetrate the opaque glaze from below during the firing, with results often indistinguishable from painting over the unfired glaze. However, some of the weaker pigments important in the Italian majolica style of the 16th century had to be applied over the glaze, and this has been the standard practice since that time.

Majolica Application. Many methods can be used for applying oxide solutions, underglaze colors, or colored glazes over a raw glaze surface. The most common is brushing; but spraying, dipping, wax resist, trailing, or printing with sponge stamps provides a wide range of possibilities.

The only serious problem in execution is that the raw glaze coating becomes very absorbent and powdery when dry. This makes brushwork with wax, oxides, or glazes very difficult, as particles of glaze tend to ball up on the brush, making any fluid strokes impossibile. The excessive absorbency also makes application of a second glaze by dipping, pouring, trailing, or printing hazardous, as the dry undercoat absorbs moisture from the wet glaze too rapidly, resulting in an application which is too thick and may crack and fall off in drying or even loosen the undercoat, leading to crawling in the firing.

The simplest way to avoid these difficulties is to decorate soon after glazing while the base coat still retains some moisture but is dry enough to handle. The time span depends on the hardness of the bisque, size of the piece, thickness of the glaze coating, and humidity and temperature of the air. I usually find that the glaze presents a good working surface for wax or oxide solution brushwork from 15 minutes to one or two hours after applying the base coat by dipping or pouring. For applying a second glaze, the time span is shorter. This should be done as soon as the first coat is dry enough to handle.

Glaze Binders. Some glazes become more powdery than others upon drying, and if this is a problem there are a number of materials which when added in small amounts to the glaze batch will produce a tougher, less powdery dry coat. The traditional binders are gum arabic and gum tragacanth (saps exuded from various acacia trees and leguminous herbs, respectively). The gums are normally available in dry powder form or in ready-to-use solutions. The powder is prepared for use by dissolving it in a small amount of alcohol, then mixing with water to a thin, custardlike consistency. A few drops of oil of cloves or formaldehyde will prevent or retard spoilage. About 2 to 6 tablespoons of gum solution per gallon of glaze is normally used. The problem of spoilage can be avoided altogether by using a synthetic gum solution such as methocel or an acrylic medium. About 2 to 6 tablespoons of acrylic medium per quart of glaze produces a very tough dry coat.

A small amount of sugar, dextrin, or syrup added to the glaze forms a thin crust on the surface of the glaze as it dries. As these will ferment, however, they are not practical for adding to large batches to be used over a long period.

Perhaps the simplest solution is to spray a thin film of gum arabic over the dry glaze. A small bulb atomizer can be used for this. When dry, the film provides a good working surface and does not prevent adhesion of colorants or glaze.

All of these binders burn out in the firing and have no effect on the fired glaze.

Majolica Colors. Majolica decoration is usually done over a white or very light-colored glaze, because this provides a neutral background against which the colored patterns stand out boldly. Very beautiful and subtle effects can be obtained, however, when glaze and decoration colors are close in value. It must be remembered, however, that some colorants are also fluxes, and the combination of colorants in glaze and decoration may cause running and blurring. Also, colorants in the glaze will combine with, and may radically change, the colorants in the decoration. Colorants will appear quite different over different white base glazes and in different thicknesses. In a cone 10 reduction firing, red iron oxide over a white glaze may appear pale green, green-brown, brown, yellow, red-brown, red-orange, or metallic black depending on the composition of the base glaze, the thickness of the iron itself, and the amount of reduction.

Metallic oxides and commercial underglaze

Hispano-Moresque tin-glazed earthenware dish with cobalt and luster decoration. Spain (Manises), 420–30. The Metropolitan Museum of Art: the Cloisters Collection.

owl decorated in black slip under turquoise glaze, Persia. Fitzwilliam Museum, Cambridge, Mass.

(Left) Majolica urn, blue with luster decoration. Italy (Deruta). Victoria and Albert Museum.

Bowl with incised decoration accented with colored glazes. Persia. British Museum.

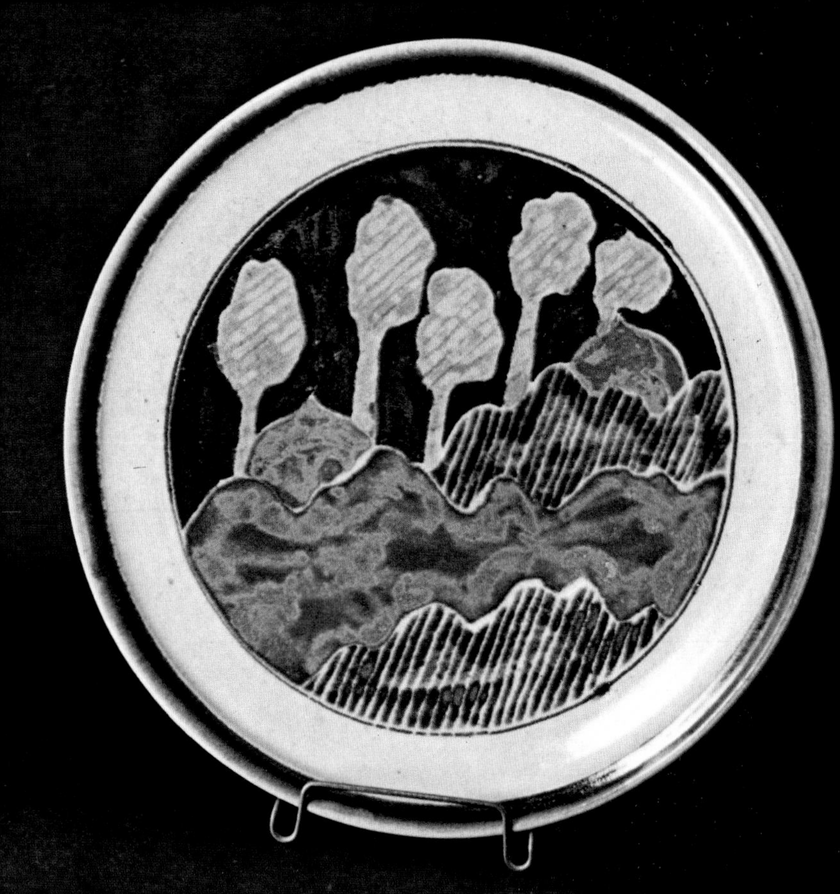

Stoneware plate with wax-resist decoration, 18″ in diameter. John Fassbinder, U.S.A. Courtesy of the College of Wooster.

Stoneware bowl with decoration trailed in blue glaze on bisque under sprayed white glaze. Workshop of Wilhelm and Elly Kuch, Germany, 1974.

Majolica dish. Spanish, early 20th century. Collection of the author.

Porcelain plate with cobalt decoration under transparent glaze, iron-red, green, and yellow overglaze, gold luster, 18" in diameter. Ralph Bacerra, U.S.A.

Porcelain plate with scalloped rim, cobalt decoration under transparent glaze, iron-red and green overglaze, gold luster, 11" in diameter. Ralph Bacerra, U.S.A.

(Right) Covered jar with colored lead glazes. China, T'ang dynasty. British Museum.

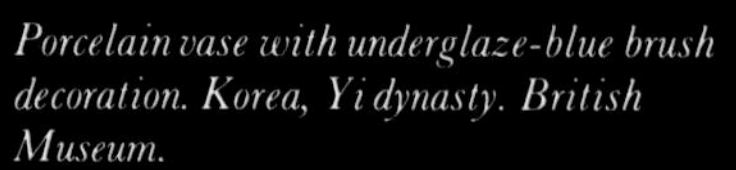

Porcelain vase with underglaze-blue brush decoration. Korea, Yi dynasty. British Museum.

Porcelain vase, wheelthrown with poured slab lattice. Kurt and Gerda Spurey, Austria, 1971.

(Right) Detail, slab-built stoneware bottle, by the author, 1965. The relief pattern was formed by pressing clay into a cardboard egg-cratelike panel.

(Far right) Detail, slab-built box, by the author, 1968. The raised decoration is formed of tiny coils with bright-colored cone 06 glazes applied after stoneware firing.

(Right) Detail, bowl with wax-resist decoration over raw glaze, by the author, 1972.

(Far right) Detail, bowl with stamped and combed decoration. James McKinnell, U.S.A.

Stoneware covered jar, sgraffito through white slip under transparent glaze. Blue underglaze, yellow, orange, and green overglaze decoration, 18" in diameter, 7" high. Ralph Bacerra, U.S.A.

Stoneware pilgrim bottle with impressed decoration, by the author, 1974.

(Left) Covered jar with decoration on white-slip ground under clear glaze. Turkey (Iznik), late 16th century. British Museum.

Salt-glazed stoneware covered jar with sprigged decoration. Les Miley, U.S.A.

(Right) Porcelain covered jar, black and white cone 10 glazes, airbrushed pink and pearl lusters over platinum luster. Susanne Stephenson, U.S.A.

(Far right) Stoneware covered jar with brush decoration over raw glaze. Robert Sperry, U.S.A., 1966.

Salt-glazed porcelain plate with paper-stencil and sgraffito decoration. Don Pilcher, U.S.A.

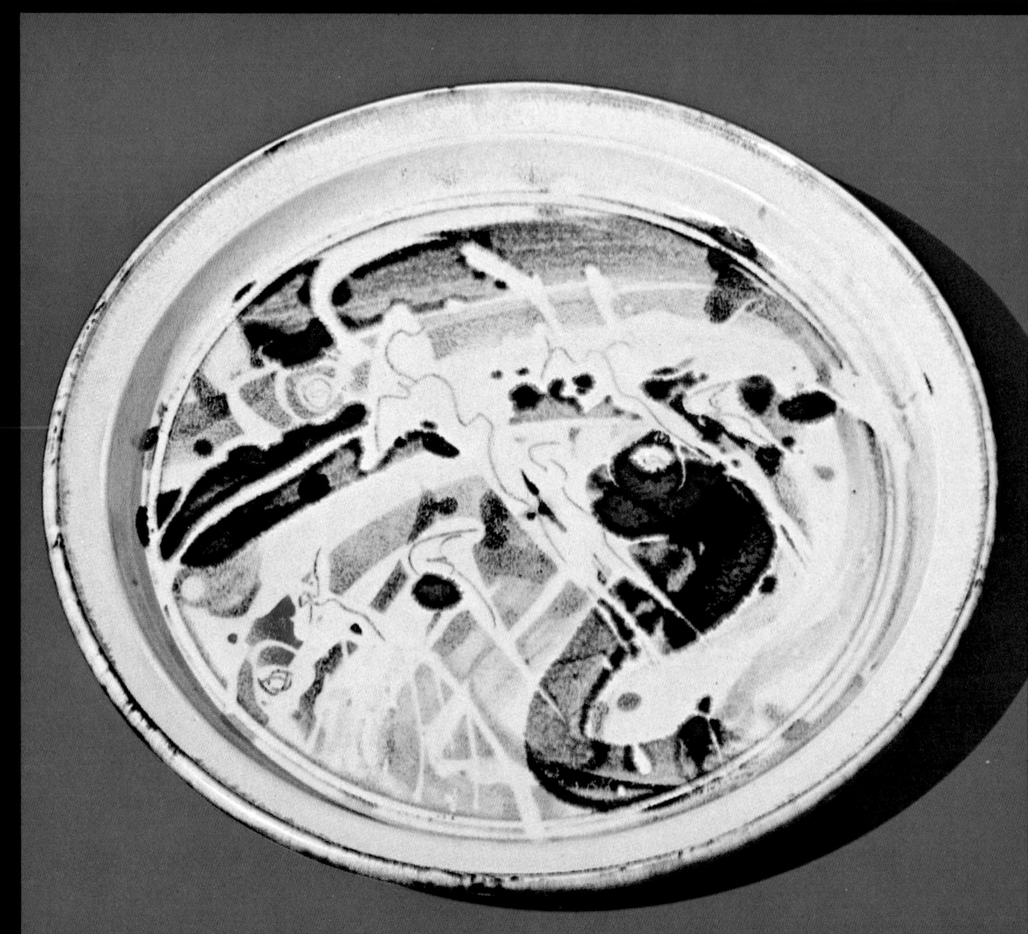

Porcelain plate with wax-resist, sgraffito, and brush decoration over raw glaze. James McKinnell, U.S.A.

"Made in U.S.A.," Slab-built, cone 6 oxidation stoneware plate with multiple-process decoration: stamping, slip trailing, photo silkscreen, underglaze, underglaze pencil, and airbrush. Les Lawrence, U.S.A.

Stoneware bowl with wax-resist decoration, by the author.

ft) Bottle with incised decora-
. Stig Lyndberg, Sweden.

(Right) Porcelain bottle with
brush decoration. Wilhelm and
Elly Kuch, Germany, 1974.

Far right) Porcelain bottle with
rush decoration. Rochester Folk
Art Guild, U.S.A.

(Right) Slab-built stoneware
ottle with impressed decoration,
by the author, 1974.

Far right) Stoneware covered jar
ith iron and cobalt brush decoration. Robert Sperry, 1966.

Plate with slip-trailed decoration on a white-slip ground, 20″ in diameter. Thomas Toft, England, late 17th century.

Stoneware plate with white-slip decora-

Hispano-Moresque dish, 17¾″ in diameter. Spain, Mainses, middle of 15th century. Victoria and Albert Museum. This dish shows the wonderful sense of design, skillful and lively brushwork and opulent color and richness for which the blue and luster ware of Manises was known throughout Western Europe in the 15th century.

colors (see Underglaze Pigments earlier in this chapter) can simply be mixed with water for painting over the glaze. It is almost impossible to give more than a rough idea of proper proportions of colorant to water as there are so many variables. The method of application, firing temperature, color tone desired, absorbency of the glaze coat, and composition of the glaze may all make changes in the ideal proportions, and the best mixtures for your purposes can be determined only through testing. (A guide to the use of some common oxides is given in the Appendix.) It is important to stir the oxide mixtures often during use as the suspended metallic particles settle rapidly. Careful handling of the unfired decorated ware is necessary because the colors smudge easily.

The use of colored glazes over the base glaze instead of watery oxide solutions may give more controllable, predictable results as it is easier to gauge thickness of application. Glazes viscous enough for dipping or pouring are, however, too thick for good brushwork on a raw glaze surface. The percentage of colorant can be increased to retain desired tinting strength in a thinned glaze. Some potters simply add a small amount of the base glaze to oxide solutions.

Glazes used for decoration should be tested for compatibility with the undercoat glaze. It is safest and most predictable to use the same glaze as undercoat and as base for the colored decorative glazes, but the interaction of different glazes in the firing can produce unexpectedly beautiful and dramatic results.

Majolica bowl. Italy (Orvieto), 15th century. Fitzwilliam Museum. The decoration on a white tin-lead glaze is outlined in manganese brown, which retains its crispness, and areas are filled in with copper green, which spreads and becomes fuzzy in the firing. This combination was also used in Spain, notably in Paterna and Teruel.

BRUSH DECORATION

Brush application of slips, underglaze, or overglaze colorants or one glaze over another is one of the most basic, yet potentially richest and most lyrical forms of decoration. There is opportunity for endless subtle variety through skillful use of different types of brushes. One of the most versatile is the bamboo-handled, pointed-tip Japanese calligraphy brush called a *fude*, which is made in many sizes. Each brush is made from at least two kinds of bristles: pig bristles to form a stiff, springy core, surrounded by softer, finer hairs to give suppleness and form a delicate point.

A medium-size *fude* holds a good supply of liquid and can be used for fine, delicate lines or broad, sweeping strokes. To get the best results with this type of brush and fully utilize its potential requires a skill which combines precise control with fluid spontaneity. The best work has a seemingly effortless natural grace which comes only with mastery of technique. The quick, free brushwork seen on many Chinese and Japanese pots may appear deceptively simple, its natural, graceful beauty easily achieved with a certain flair and boldness combined with luck. This has led to much thoughtless, sloppy, and meaningless use of Japanese brushes for pseudo-oriental decoration.

It may not be practical or meaningful for a Western potter to study in detail the complex, precise conventions of oriental painting and calligraphy on which the seemingly effortless brushwork is based, but he should attempt through practice to gain an understanding and control of his brushes. Perhaps it is best to begin with simple, contained, repetitive patterns, gradually working toward greater free-

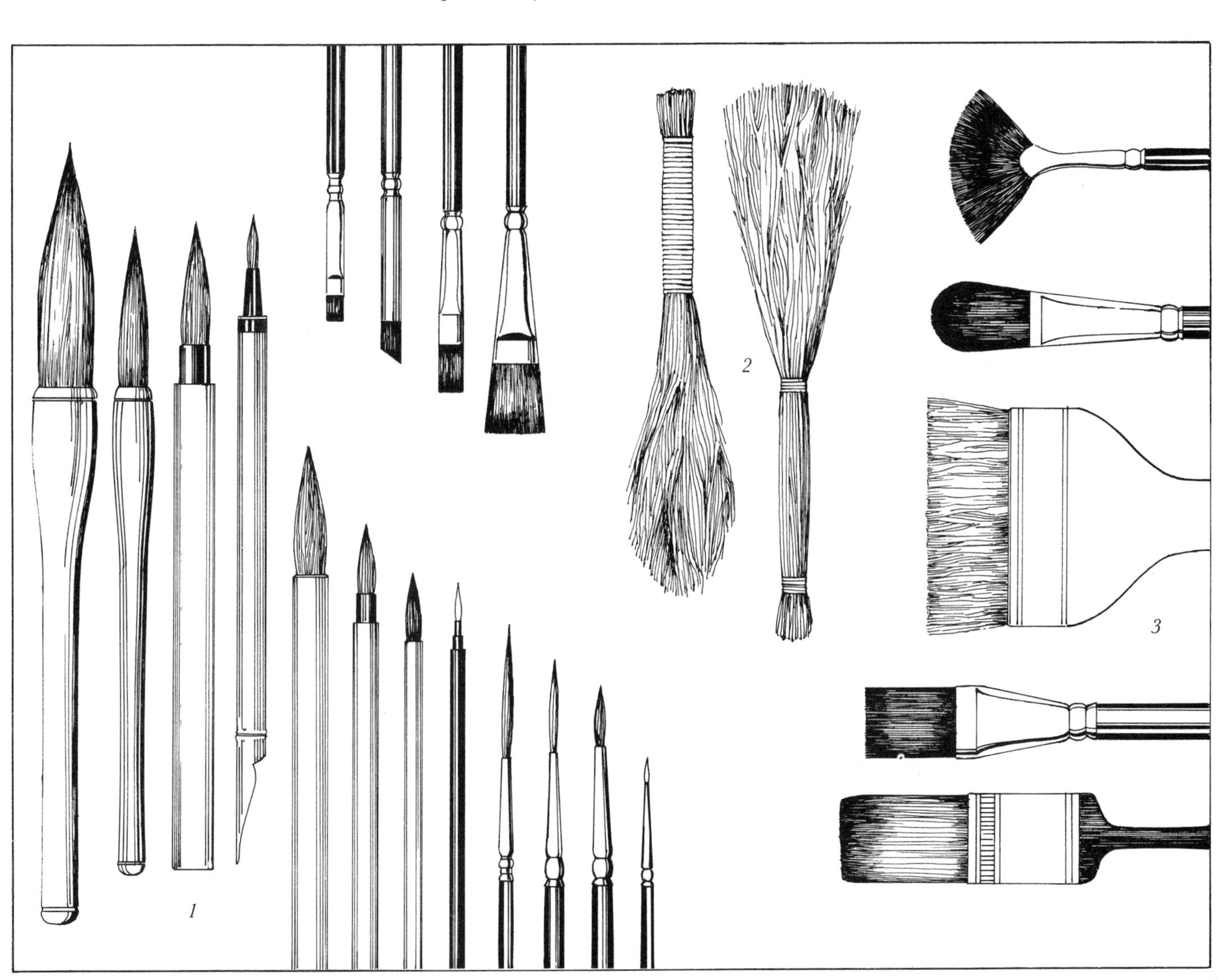

Among the brush types shown here are the Japanese brushes (1) fude, (2) hakeme, (3) hake.

dom and fluidity. Practicing simple strokes on newsprint may be helpful in developing control and confidence without tightness. Good-quality brushes can make a big difference and are well worth a little extra investment.

Other types of brushes can be used for different types of decorative effects. Broad, square, flat brushes are best for quickly and smoothly coating large areas with slip. Very thin, pointed brushes with long, soft, flexible bristles make varied, sinuous, though not completely controllable lines. Two types of brushes used by Japanese potters for making patterns in freshly applied wet slip are the *hake*, a wide, square, short-bristled brush used for patting, and the *hakeme*, a coarse, stiff rice-straw brush like a tiny rough broom, used for making irregular sweeping striations in a slip coating. Both of these very subtle techniques, usually done in white slip over a dark body, are often used as a background for bolder decoration with dark slip or oxides.

Oribe ewer. Japan, Momoyama period, 1568–1615 A.D. Freer Gallery of Art. Oribe decoration, with its splashes of green glaze and meandering, idiosyncratic brushwork in iron brown, seems determinedly erratic and whimsical—studied in its odd juxtapositions and brash coarseness—but still it remains fresh, spontaneous, often surprising, and almost always delightful.

Stoneware teapot. John Glick, U.S.A., 1973. The decoration, applied with brush and sponge print, skips playfully and somewhat erratically over the surface with unusual and delightful results.

Stoneware covered jar. Ralph Bacerra, U.S.A. Collection of Ken Deavers. Vigorous, sweeping brushstrokes embrace a full, round form in a casual, yet dramatic way.

Stoneware covered jar. Tom Mason, U.S.A., 1964. The strong, heavy-shouldered, vigorously thrown form is appropriately accented by two strokes of a wide, flat brush.

Majolica goblet. Alan Caiger-Smith, England, 1972. Alan Caiger-Smith's decoration is characterized by bold, lyrical use of both broad and pointed brushes.

Stoneware vase, 12½" high. Petr Svoboda, Czechoslovakia, 1970. The crisp, graceful form is beautifully accented by bold, sweeping brush decoration in deep cobalt blue.

Stoneware bottle. Wilhelm and Elly Kuch, Germany. This bottle is decorated in iron red on a black glaze, but instead of flowing easily with the form, the brushwork establishes a dynamic tension through its quick, staccato quality and its asymmetrical placement.

SGRAFFITO

Incised decoration cut through a coating of slip to expose the clay of contrasting color underneath is called sgraffito (also spelled "sgraffiato," meaning "scratched" in Italian). This may be a purely linear decoration, or areas may be scraped away.

This type of decoration flourished in Italy in the 15th and 16th centuries alongside the more colorful and fashionable majolica. A white-slip ground, tinged ivory by a lead glaze, contrasts beautifully with the warm red of the clay body. Although sometimes enlivened with splashes of pale green, brown, blue, or yellow transparent glaze, softening the red-white color contrast, the crisp clarity of the incising still comes through.

The technique can be traced back through Byzantium to Syria and Persia where a variety of exceptionally beautiful sgraffito ware was made during the 9th to 13th centuries. The designs were most often cut through a white engobe, exposing a dark body, but sometimes they were scratched through a black slip over a light body. Transparent glazes were turquoise, pale green, or clear with splashes of green, yellow, or brown. The designs are sometimes subtle and restrained, sometimes delightfully bizarre with fanciful animals and stylized foliage patterns completely covering the piece.

Some of the most impressive achievements in the sgraffito technique are the vigorous yet graceful Tz'u Chou wares of Sung dynasty China. Some of these are delicately incised and covered with a transparent glaze. Others are bold combinations of incised line and cutaway areas, with no covering glaze, the dark brown or black slip melting just enough to

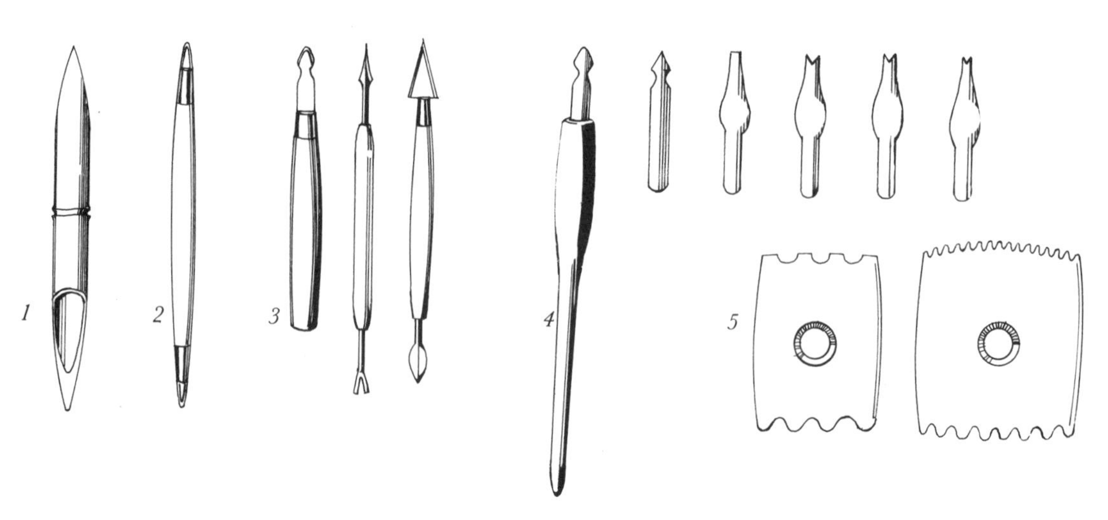

These sgraffito tools include (1) bamboo tool, (2) wire loop tool, (3) metal-bladed tools, (4) wood holder with interchangeable blades, and (5) wood combs.

Using a very small wire loop tool, a sgraffito design is outlined in a firm, but still-damp slip coating on the leather-hard pot.

Areas of slip are easily scraped away with a larger loop tool.

form a buttery matt glaze, making a dramatic contrast with the rough, unglazed areas.

Sgraffito is normally done when the piece is leatherhard and the slip coating is still a little damp but dry enough to be handled without damage. At this stage the tool cuts smoothly, leaving a clean, sharp line. A quite different character may be achieved by cutting through wetter or dryer slip. If the slip is wet, a smooth, liquid line with slight ridges along the edges results; if the slip is dry, the line will be fuzzy or ragged.

Special sgraffito tools may be purchased which have flat or spoon-shaped blades with pointed, square, or rounded tips. With these it is possible to cut fine or broad lines cleanly without digging deeply into the clay. Good tools can be improvised or made from metal or wood, the ideal material and shape depending on whether the tool is used with wet, firm, or dry slip and on the potter's manner of working and desired results. Commercial wire or spring-steel loop tools are very useful, especially for cutting away areas between lines.

Glaze Sgraffito. Although sgraffito is a technique usually employed with slip, it can also be effective when done through a viscous glaze. The decoration should be done on freshly applied glaze (as soon as it is firm enough to handle) to avoid ragged, chipped edges. If completely dry, the glaze tends to chip much more easily; sometimes even large areas may fall off. Very delicate, subtle effects can be obtained if the glaze melts in the firing just enough to soften the line. If the glaze becomes too fluid in firing, fine lines may be completely sealed over and disappear.

Stoneware jug. Michael Cardew, England. Victoria and Albert Museum. The linear patterns are cut through a coat of dark slip glaze to reveal the body.

Earthenware dish, 12¼″ in diameter. Persia, 12th century. Although similar in materials, color, and technique to the Italian bowl above, the character of this piece is quite different because of the loose, asymmetrical composition.

Shallow bowl, 14″ in diameter. Italy (Tuscany or Umbria), early 16th century. Victoria and Albert Museum. The sgraffito decoration is crisply and cleanly cut through a white slip to reveal a red body. The bowl is covered with a clear glaze, with touches of pale brown and grayish blue glazes on the bird and its star-shaped frame.

Stoneware bottle, 13¾″ high. China, Tzu-chou, Sung dynasty, 960–1279 A.D. Cleveland Museum of Art, Purchase, J.H. Wade Fund. The decoration is vigorously carved through a dark slip band into the wall of the pot.

SLIP TRAILING

Slip trailing is a process by which slip is forced through a small aperture to deposit a raised line, usually of contrasting color to the clay of the pot. Some of the best and most famous examples of this technique are the large plates made by potters in Staffordshire, England, in the late 17th century. The pieces were first coated with a white slip; then the designs were trailed in red and brown slips, accented with white dots on the brown lines; finally the whole plate was covered with a transparent-yellow lead glaze. There is usually a figurative subject—a mermaid combing her hair, the temptation of Adam and Eve, "The Pelican in Her Piety" (depicting a pelican wounding herself to feed her young, symbolizing Christ's sacrifice), cavaliers and ladies, royal portraits and coats of arms, enriched with scroll, floral, and lattice patterns. A popular theme after the restoration of Charles II in 1660 was "Prince Charles in the Oak" (shown at top of page 112) a symbolic representation of an incident occurring in 1651 when Charles, fleeing from Cromwell's soldiers, hid for a day in a large oak tree. Only Charles' head appears in the tree, flanked by symbols of royalty, the lion and the unicorn. As the potter's bold signature often forms a part of the decoration, it is clear that many of the finest slipware plates were made by Thomas Toft. His ability as a draftsman and his wonderful sense of composition give his work a sophistication while it still retains a robust, naïve quality. The trailed line of English slipware decoration is smooth, continuous, and of even thickness, indicating a flowing, steady manner of drawing.

Simpler in concept and showing greater verve in execution are the fanciful decorations on the strictly utilitarian salt-glazed crocks and jugs produced in potteries in New York, New England, and Ohio in the mid-19th century. In contrast to the earlier English tradition of smoothly trailed continuous lines in three colors on a wet slip background, the American potters always used cobalt-blue decoration directly on the pot. The best decorators perfected a quick stroke with a globular beginning tapering to a fine point, and developed designs of considerable complexity with great speed and flourish.

Slip Trailers. There are numerous versions of the traditional gravity-feed slip trailer. The simplest is a small, usually glazed, ceramic bottle shape made to fit comfortably in the potter's hand. There are two openings: one for filling and a narrow spout with a tiny opening through which the slip runs when the vessel is tipped. Often the filling hole is so placed that it can easily be covered or uncovered with the thumb to stop or start the flow of slip. Many old slip cups have a quill inserted in the trailing spout for a finer flow. Another style uses a quill inserted in a cork which plugs one of the two openings in the vessel. Two or more parallel lines can be trailed at once by a slip cup fitted with multiple quills. The Pennsylvania Germans used vessels with two to five quills and occasionally even seven. Parallel lines of different colors can be made by trailers with two or more separate compartments, each with its own quill. Maintaining an even flow of slip was always a problem, and one English version included a long tube through which the potter could blow to create a forced flow.

A Japanese version of the slip trailer, used at Tamba for beautiful calligraphy, is made from two sections of bamboo, a thick one about 2″ in diameter for the body, with a very thin one inserted for a spout. The slip flows when the vessel is tipped like a small pitcher.

Modern rubber and plastic products designed for other purposes can be readily used or adapted for slip trailing. Flexible plastic bottles such as mustard or catsup dispensers can be used, but the best and easiest to use trailer is a small rubber syringe. A smooth flow of slip is achieved by gently but firmly squeezing the bulb. If the slip is well sieved and of the proper consistency to allow it to flow from the aperture with only a light pressure on the bulb and the bulb is refilled when it is still about ⅓ full, there should be no problem with sudden spurts caused by lumpy slip or air pockets.

The size of the hole may be reduced by inserting a tiny plastic tube (a short section of electric wire insulation). For very fine work, a further reduction can be made by inserting a still smaller tube into the first one. The smaller the hole, of course, the thinner the slip must be to maintain a smooth flow.

The slip for trailing must be very smooth and should be sieved through an 80- or 100-mesh screen. Some potters add a little gum tragacanth to improve flow and adhesion. Slip used in a rubber bulb or a flexible plastic bottle can be a little thicker than in the gravity-feed type, which is an advantage on shapes where the slip is likely to run. Flat shapes such as plates or rectangular bottles which can be held horizontally while decorating are easiest for trailing, but with practice, other shapes can be handled.

It is a good idea to practice on a clay slab which can be scraped clean and reused before working on actual pots. The trailer should be small and easily held in one hand. The movement must be smooth and fluid; every hesitation leaves a blob. Mastering the sinuous, flowing lines characteristic of good slip trailing requires considerable practice, but once the necessary speed, confidence, and control have been achieved, it is a uniquely satisfying technique to use.

Although usually a form of color decoration, trailing can be used purely for its inherent tactile quality as sculptural decoration by using a slip made of the body clay. This may or may not be accented later with oxides or slips or with a glaze which breaks into a different color where it runs thin on the ridges.

Trailed-Slip Transfer. The slip-trailing technique can be varied for slab construction by making the slip design on a board or large plaster bat. When the slip has stiffened somewhat, a wet slab is laid over it and rolled with a rolling pin. This, of course, results in a flat surface similar in appearance to an inlay, rather than the raised line characteristic of slip trailing. There is some distortion of the line as the slab is pressed onto it, but this can produce interesting though uncontrollable results. Trailing may also be done in a plaster mold into which slabs will later be pressed.

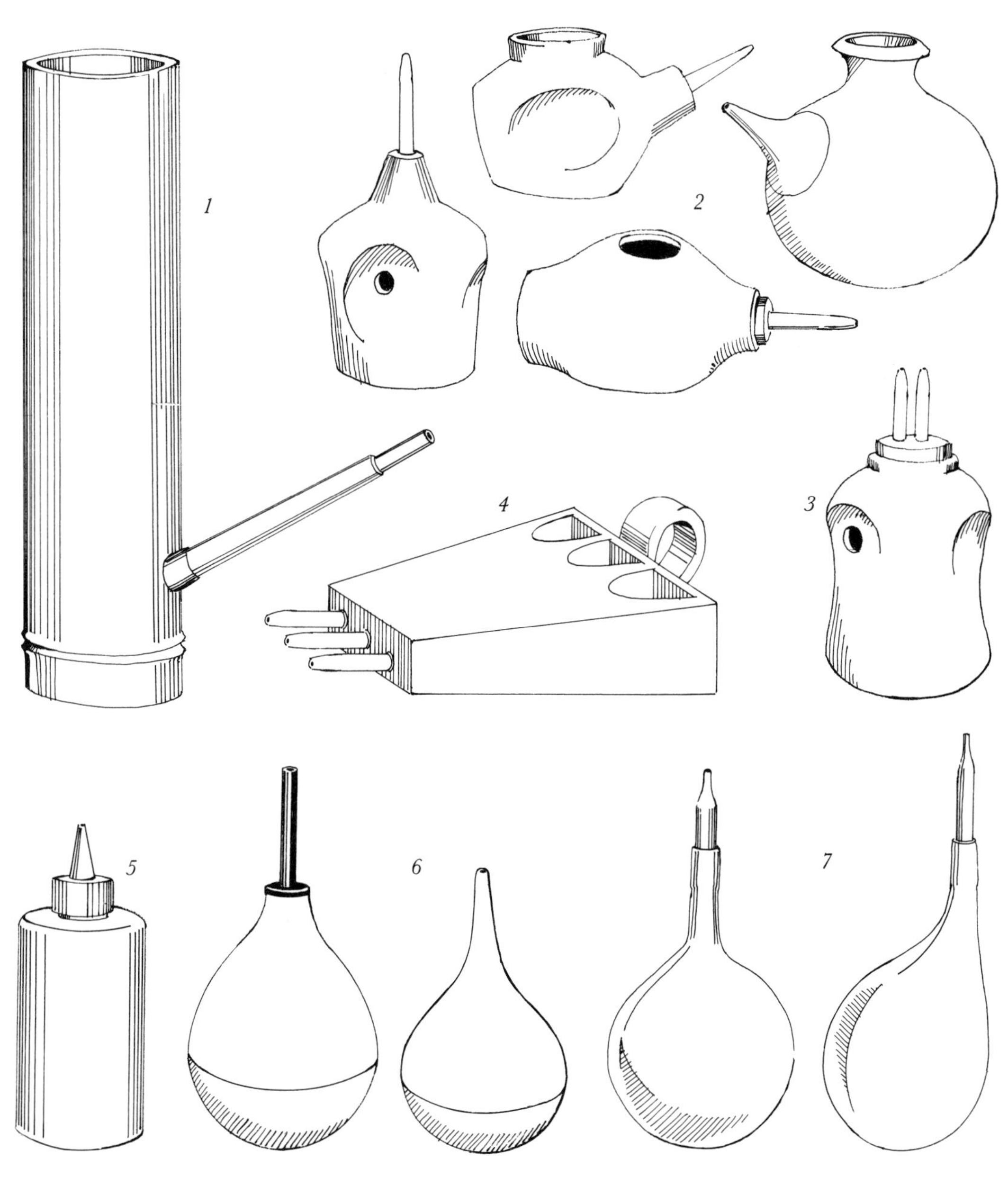

These slip trailers include (1) bamboo, (2) clay, (3) double-quill, (4) triple-compartment, (5) plastic bottle, (6) rubber syringes, (7) soft rubber bulb with glass tube.

Large stoneware storage jar. Ralph Bacerra, U.S.A. Collection of Ken Deavers. The basic design is sgraffito through a green slip revealing a buff body. Details are added in trailed white slip.

Salt-glazed stoneware crock, 11½" high x 11½" in diameter, 4 gallon capacity. Albany, New York, 19th century. New York State Historical Association, Cooperstown. The dynamic bird is built up with swift, tapering, trailed strokes in deep cobalt blue.

GLAZE TRAILING

Trailing can be done with glazes on bisque ware in the same way slip trailing is done on damp pots. It is, however, difficult to glaze pieces so decorated by pouring or dipping without spoiling the decoration. Interior surfaces of bottles, jars, etc., can be poured before decorating, but the glaze over the trailing is best applied by spraying. Glaze trailing can also be done over an unfired dry glaze coat, but this may involve some problems with the thick, trailed decoration lifting off as it dries.

The trailed glaze line melts into the glaze surface rather than remaining as a raised line as slip does. If the trailed glaze is sufficiently refractory, however, the quality of the stroke will remain clear. Some glazes, especially those with iron as a colorant, tend to bleed and spread in the firing, so that the character of the trailed line is dissipated.

Mugs. Kuch Workshop, Germany, 1974. These mugs have been bisque fired, then decorated with trailed glaze. A white glaze will be sprayed over the decoration. Much of the standard ware of the workshop is decorated in this way. Although decorating is done by several different people, a common vocabulary of design motifs and a common technique using short, quick, tapering strokes to build up complex patterns results in an identifiable workshop style, while allowing considerable variation and improvisation.

Glaze trailing with a rubber syringe.

The incised or impressed patterns are filled with thick slip. A second coat may be needed to completely fill the depressions. When the slip has hardened to the same consistency as the clay body, the surface is scraped, leaving slip only in the incised or impressed patterns.

Stoneware bowl. Korean, Koryo Dynasty. Freer Gallery of Art. This exceptionally elaborate and delicate mishima bowl is inlaid with white and black slip under a pale-green celadon glaze.

MISHIMA

Mishima is a slip-inlay technique, most closely associated with Korean pottery of the Koryo dynasty (918–1392 A.D.). Between 1000 and 1300 A.D. the Korean potters developed and refined the technique to produce decoration of intricate complexity while preserving, through restraint and sublety of form and color, great dignity and serenity. A pale-gray firing clay was used, into which the decoration was incised, combed, or impressed with small stamps. The depressions were filled with white slip or a combination of white and black (the white slip, itself, sometimes inlaid with black), creating very sharp, clean patterns which showed clearly through a transparent pale gray or gray-green celadon glaze.

Mishima is the name given by the Japanese to this Korean ware when it was imported. According to an old tradition, the delicate inlay decoration resembled the calligraphic characters in the almanacs compiled at a monastery in the town of Mishima, but the name may derive from the tiny islands called Mishima, where ships traveling between Korea and Japan could have stopped.

The incising or stamping can be done in soft to leatherhard clay, and should not be very deep. Japanese potters often use a sharpened V- or U-shaped umbrella stay as a carving tool, plowing a neat, clean line in the manner of wood or copper engraving.

The depressions are filled with very thick slip, either by brushing it into the depressions, or simply coating the entire decorated area. When the slip has stiffened to the same consistency as the body—ideally about leatherhard—the piece is lightly scraped with a flexible metal rib or other tool, leaving slip only in the incised or impressed designs. These areas must be completely filled with slip to make a level surface. A smooth clay body without coarse grog works best, as the incising and scraping tend to tear out coarse particles.

Two or more colors can be inlaid at once or in successive operations, one color even inlaid in another after the first has stiffened.

Stoneware bottle. Korean, Koryo dynasty. Freer Gallery of Art. The delicate patterns were incised in the gray clay body, then inlaid with white slip and covered with an olive-green celadon glaze.

FEATHER COMBING AND MARBLING

The techniques of feather combing and marbling were popular in England and America in the 18th and 19th centuries. Of the two, feather combing is more controlled and subtle. Marbling may completely dominate the form with its beautiful swirling patterns. As these are largely a matter of chance, they may seem unrelated to the form, especially if slips of strongly contrasting colors are used.

Feather combing and marbling are liquid-slip techniques usually done on flat, wet clay slabs. After a slab and its slip coating have stiffened it can be formed into a bowl or plate on a hump mold or used in slab construction. As the slip must be applied in a thick liquid coat, it is difficult to work on an inclined or vertical surface, although the inside of a still-wet, shallow thrown bowl or plate provides a good surface. The clay should be quite damp so that the slip will remain liquid during the decorating process.

In practice, for both feather combing and marbling, slip of one color is poured over the entire slab or area to be decorated, covering it with a thick, even coat. Using a rubber syringe or other slip trailer, lines are then trailed across the slab with one or more slips of contrasting colors. The patterns resulting from feather combing or marbling are most interesting when there is variety in the spacing and thickness of the trailed lines.

The wet slip is jarred by bumping the board on the table once or twice, causing the trailed lines to sink in level with the background. For feather combing, the tip of a feather, a broomstraw, or other fine, flexible point is drawn lightly back and forth across the lines of slip, leaving no incision itself but delicately pulling one color into the next.

Marbled effects may be achieved by tilting and sharply shaking or twisting the slip-covered slab either before or after combing, causing the colored slips to run into irregular swirling lines and resulting in surprising, sometimes very beautiful patterns. This technique is sometimes used to improve combed designs which have not turned out well.

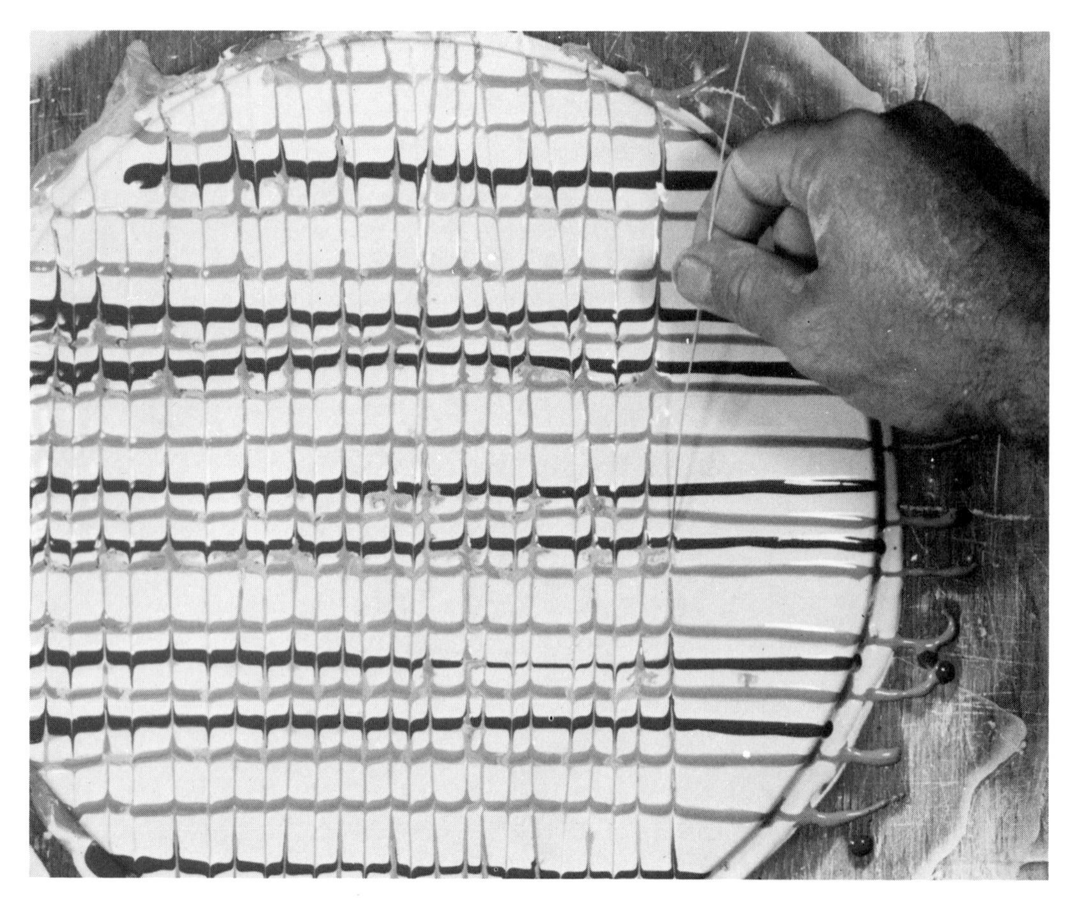

The slab is first given a thick coat of white slip, then lines of one or more slips of contrasting colors are trailed across the still-liquid surface. The slab is jarred so that the trailed lines sink level with the surface. The tip of a feather, a broom straw, or other thin, flexible point (a potter's needle tool is too stiff) is drawn lightly across the lines of liquid slip.

Marbled bowl. England, early 18th century. Victoria and Albert Museum. Dark-brown slip was trailed on a ground of wet white slip and the dish then jarred and twisted, causing the slip to flow into irregular swirling patterns.

Wax resist on raw glaze surface. After the liquid wax design has hardened, metallic oxide colorants brushed over the surface are repelled by the wax, reserving the design in the glaze color.

Bowl, wax-resist decoration. Alan Caiger-Smith, England. The coloring oxide was applied by holding the charged brush lightly against the raw-glaze surface as the bowl turned on the wheel.

WAX RESIST

When a pattern of liquid wax is applied to a pot and allowed to harden, glaze, slip, or oxide colorants applied over it will adhere only to the unwaxed areas. The wax itself is burned away in the firing. Wax resist can be used on leatherhard pots in conjunction with slips or underglaze colorants, on bisque ware to reserve a pattern of unglazed clay, or over raw glaze with oxides or another glaze.

Beeswax, paraffin, or mixtures of paraffin and kerosene (varying from 1 to 1 to 3 to 1), which must be heated to make them fluid, have traditionally been used for resist, but the emulsion-type wax sold by ceramic supply houses is more convenient and easier to use, and produces equally good results. Wax emulsion can be thinned with water and should be just thick enough to repel the slip, colorant, or glaze used over it. If too thick, it does not brush on smoothly and stays tacky too long after application. If too thin, it will not repel cleanly and completely, leaving a shaggy, blotchy pattern. Ideally only a few drops of colorant will cling to the waxed areas and if a clean, precise pattern is wanted, these can be removed by blowing on the area, forcing the drops off the wax, or by blotting with a damp paper towel or fine sponge. In many cases, however, it may be preferable to leave them for a softer effect.

Wax Over Raw Glaze. On leatherhard clay the wax emulsion takes a long time to dry, but on bisque ware or over raw glaze, it takes only about 5 to 30 minutes depending on the thickness of the wax and the amount of moisture still in the glaze. When used over a raw glaze, the waxing can be done as soon as the glaze is dry to the touch and should be completed within an hour or two after glazing. When the glaze becomes completely dry, it is impossible to do any good brushwork as the brush picks up particles of glaze from the powdery surface, producing a very rough, shaggy pattern. For the same reason, colorants should be applied as soon as the wax is dry. Use of a binder in the glaze will produce a tougher, less powdery dry coat. (See Glaze Binders earlier in this chapter.)

If the piece is to have a second layer of glaze over the wax pattern, it is especially important to complete the process before the initial glaze coating is completely dry. Otherwise the piece will take on a too-thick layer of the second glaze which may crack and flake off as it dries, or even cause loosening of the undercoat and consequent blistering or crawling in the firing. Spraying the second glaze can produce a thinner coating, but when sprayed the glaze is not repelled cleanly by the wax. Liquid latex will give better results.

Heated paraffin has the advantage of drying immediately upon application and it is possible by using it to do even two or three successive layers of wax and glaze. Decoration of great depth and richness may be built up by first brushing on a pattern in one color, followed by a wax pattern in another color, more wax, and a third color.

It may be desirable to sketch roughly the proposed decoration before applying the wax. This may be done lightly with a soft pencil or with a brush using a thin ink solution, which will burn out in the firing.

Liquid Latex. Liquid latex can be used instead of wax. Sold in paste form, it is thinned with water to a creamy consistency. The latex pattern can be easily peeled off after application of color to leave a perfectly clean pattern. This makes it excellent as a resist for sprayed colors and also makes it possible to correct mistakes easily or to apply a glaze over the decoration.

Cuerda Seca. Various waxy or oily substances have been used for resist decoration. An interesting example is the *cuerda seca* (dry line) technique used in Spain in Medieval and Renaissance periods. A linear pattern was applied with a brush using a mixture of linseed or other oil and manganese. Glazes of various colors were then applied to the spaces between the lines, the colors neatly contained by the oily lines. The effect is rather like a mosaic, with areas of color outlined by dry, black lines, and in fact the technique was quite successfully used on tiles to imitate intricate ceramic mosaics. Wax can also be used in this way, the wax carrying its own color, rather than reserving areas of the underlying color.

Sgraffito and Wax. The sgraffito technique may be used with wax, with the entire piece or certain areas simply waxed and the actual decoration done by scratching through the wax coating, then brushing over the scratched design with a colorant. Scratched lines may also be linear embellishments of a basic wax pattern.

Stoneware bottle, about 15" high. Shoji Hamada, Japan, about 1931. Victoria and Albert Museum. The vigorous, eloquent wax-resist brushwork and the simple, robust form are typical of Hamada's work.

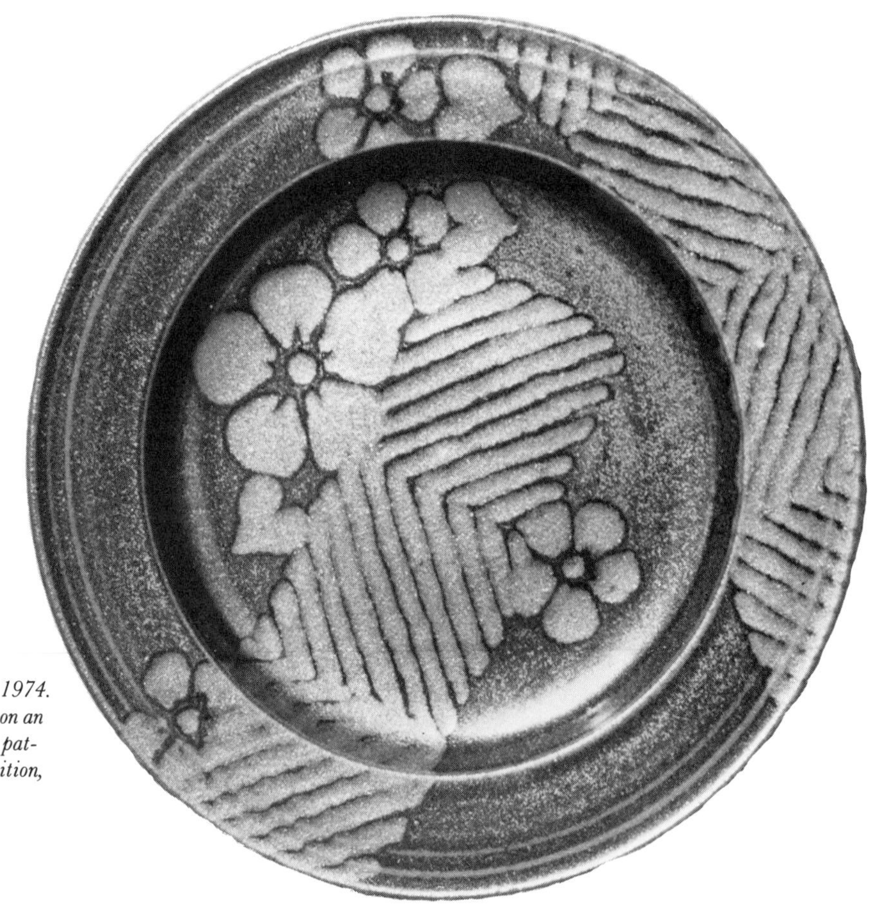

Stoneware plate. Michael Cohen, 1974. The decoration in brilliant orange on an iron-red glaze is printed with four patterned sponges, a dramatic composition, simply and quickly executed.

Stoneware plate, 14" in diameter. James McKinnell, U.S.A. An iron slip was applied over a wax and sgraffito design.

STAMP PRINTING AND LIFT-OFF

The use of stamps for printing colorants on raw glaze or removing part of a wet slip coating can produce rich and complex patterns very quickly. Considerable variety is possible through different combinations of a few small stamps.

For printing with oxides over a raw glaze, stamps made of very fine-textured artificial sponge or foam rubber are used. The pattern in the sponge stamp is easily made by drawing on it with a heated metal point. A soldering iron or wood-burning pen with a fine point is ideal, but a hot nail will do. In this way a line can easily be melted into the material, whereas cutting a pattern into it with a knife or scissors is almost impossible. Small pieces of sponge are easy to use, but anything over 2″ to 3″ square becomes rather awkward.

The printing should be done as soon as the glaze is dry enough to handle. The sponge is first immersed in water and squeezed out, then dipped into an oxide solution (the same watery consistency as for brushwork) and pressed lightly for just a second onto the raw glaze. It takes some experimenting to learn the amount of imprinting pressure and the proper oxide strengths for a given glaze.

The lift-off technique is done on wet or leatherhard pots with a fresh coating of slip. A patterned sponge is pressed lightly onto the wet slip, absorbing some slip and leaving a pattern of exposed clay when it is lifted off. As the slip is not cleanly and completely removed, the effect is softer and fuzzier than sgraffito.

Stamps of other porous materials such as wood, plaster, or bisque-fired clay are as good, as, if not better than, the sponge stamps for the lift-off technique on flat or simple convex surfaces. They become saturated with moisture rather quickly, however, and then must be allowed to dry out.

Various stamps have been used to remove, by absorption, part of a wet-slip coating: sponge (left), wood (bottom right), plaster (top right).

Salt-glazed porcelain plate. Don Pilcher, U.S.A. Paper stencils and heavily applied slip were used to create a powerful, dramatic design, enriched by the whimsical meandering trail of a cog wheel and vigorously modeled rim.

STENCILS

Green leaves were used as stencils by Chinese potters in the later Sung dynasty. Wet leaves were applied to the damp pot which was then dipped in slip, usually white. When the slip had stiffened, the leaves were carefully pulled off, leaving a clean pattern of bare clay, the slip retaining a sharp, slightly raised edge around the pattern. The simple stenciled patterns were sometimes embellished with brushwork or sgraffito details. Cut-out patterns, probably of paper, were also used, resulting in decoration similar to, yet subtly different from, sgraffito or wax resist.

Wet paper (thin, soft, porous paper such as newsprint or typing paper works well) will adhere to wet or leatherhard clay when pressed into place with fingers or a damp sponge. Slip or glaze can be applied over the stencil by dipping, pouring, brushing, or spraying. Thin oxide solutions may tend to soak through or seep under the edges of the stencil. The paper can be carefully lifted off as soon as the shine has left the coating or can be left until almost dry. If removed when completely dry, edges of the pattern may chip. Complex designs can be made with negative stencils or laid on in many small positive sections. Torn edges can produce an effect unobtainable with other techniques. The decoration can be carefully worked out by rearranging the component pieces before they are moistened and pressed in place.

Several layers of pattern and color can be built up by adding new stencils after the first layer of slip or glaze is firm, but not completely dry, and then applying a second coat. The process can be repeated a third time, but more than this may build up too great a thickness. The original stencils may be removed before adding more or all may be left in place until after the final coat of slip or glaze.

More durable stencils can be made from regular stencil paper or other hard, slick paper, but these are good only for flat surfaces with spray or brush application of slip or glaze. Thin oxide solutions tend to seep under the edges of heavy stencils. For use on bisque pots or over a fired glaze, stencils can be cut from gummed paper or masking tape.

Paper stencils. Cut, torn, and punched stencils of thin, soft paper were soaked in water and pressed onto the damp clay surface. Excess water was removed by wiping gently with a sponge, and a coat of white slip was applied. After the slip has stiffened, but is still damp, the stencils are removed. If carefully removed, some may be reusable, but normally they are used only once.

Soup tureen, 10½″ high. John Fassbinder, 1974. Courtesy the College of Wooster. The decoration is printed in two colors with patterned sponges over the raw glaze.

John Glick applies thick white slip to areas of the plate.

A design is made in the wet slip with a patterned sponge.

A broom-straw whisk is used for scratchy, irregular lines, somewhat similar to oriental hakeme decoration.

A plastic squeeze bottle is used for trailing.

A brush with stiff tufted bristles makes an interesting pattern.

An area of dark slip is patterned with a sponge.

Stoneware plate, 18″ in diameter. John Glick, U.S.A. Most of the techniques shown at left were used on this plate. After bisque firing, transparent glazes were applied, and iron and cobalt decoration with brush and sponge printing was done on the raw glaze surface. The overlapping layers of decoration, related only casually and informally to each other, have a fascinating depth and richness.

SEVEN

OVERGLAZE ENAMELS, LOW-TEMPERATURE GLAZES AND LUSTERS

Metallic lusters as well as many glaze colorants can only be fired at low temperatures. Lusters and overglaze enamels are applied over a fired glaze and refired usually to about cone 018. Many of the same colors can be used in cone 06 to 05 glazes, which can be applied on bisqued or fired glaze surfaces.

OVERGLAZE ENAMELS

Overglaze decoration is applied over a glaze which has already been fired to maturity. The decoration is fused onto the glaze surface in a subsequent low-temperature firing (cone 018 to 014) in contrast to majolica in which the decoration, applied on the raw glaze, fuses into the glaze as it matures. Unlike underglaze colors, which are themselves relatively nonfusible and can be used over a wide temperature range, overglaze enamels are actually colored glazes melting at low temperatures.

The chief advantage of the overglaze technique is that a wide range of low-temperature colors can be used on ware which has the hardness, durability, and quality of high-temperature firing. Very precise balancing of complex compositions and multicolor relationships is possible as the colors of the enamels are essentially the same before and after firing. Mistakes in application can easily be wiped off with an alcohol-moistened cloth.

The disadvantages are that an additional firing is required, and the fired colors are less durable than underglaze or majolica. The decoration may appear superficial, especially over warm, earthy stoneware glazes; however, the contrast in character can also be effectively used. Overglaze enamels are most often used on a white background, and for this porcelain provides an ideal bright, clean white which seems to intensify the brilliance of the colors.

Overglaze enamel decoration on a white tin glaze was used by Persian potters in the 12th century. The Mina'i (enamel in Persian) palette included red, brown, purple, gray, and black overglaze enamels, and sometimes gold leaf, used in combination with cobalt-blue, chrome-green, and manganese-brown majolica or underglaze colors. There is a resemblance to illuminated manuscripts in the carefully detailed figures representing court scenes, hunting scenes, and Persian legends, and indeed pottery was sometimes decorated by manuscript painters.

In China, overglaze enamels were first used with restraint and subtlety during the 15th century, appearing as bright jewel-like touches of soft red, green, and yellow over a basic design in underglaze blue on porcelain.

The Ch'ing dynasty (1644–1912) saw the introduction of *famille verte* (green family), a

Porcelain stem cup, underglaze blue with overglaze enamel decoration, 3½″ high. China, Ming dynasty. Freer Gallery of Art. Bright, yet soft, transparent enamel colors enliven a design outlined in underglaze blue.

bold palette of sharp, intense enamel colors composed of green, yellow, red, purple, blue, and black, and later the famille rose, a group of subtle, muted shades named for its soft pink color obtained from gold chloride and iron.

Not long after Japanese porcelain production began with the discovery of a suitable clay near Arita, overglaze enamel decoration using a bright palette of blue, turquoise green, yellow, and iron red was introduced by Kakiemon I, who took his name from Kaki (Japanese for persimmon red). Distinctive decorative styles were developed at Arita, Imari, and Kutani using overglaze enamels in combination with underglaze blue on porcelain.

Ralph Bacerra follows the oriental tradition of combining cobalt blue decoration under a transparent glaze with red, green, yellow, and orange overglaze enamels and gold luster, to create complex patterns with bold, dynamic color juxtapositions (see the color section).

Overglaze enamels have not always been applied over clear-glazed white bodies or white glazes. Lajvardina ware made in Persia in the 13th and 14th centuries employed opaque white, red, and black enamels thickly applied in ornate scrollwork and geometric patterns over dark-blue or turquoise glazes. At the Bavarian pottery center of Kreussen, opaque enamels were used for decoration over traditional salt-glazed forms in the 17th century. But in both cases the enamel colors lack the brightness and liveliness which a white ground, especially porcelain, seems to provide.

Preparation and Application of Overglaze Colors. Commercially prepared overglaze colors are mixtures of low-temperature frits, coloring oxides, and sometimes opacifiers ground to a powder. As they are consistent and dependable and are available in a wide range of colors, it is rarely worthwhile for an individual potter to attempt to make his own. The commercial colors are quite expensive, but are normally used in very small amounts.

Overglaze colors are available in powder form which is prepared for painting by mixing with a medium, usually fat oil of turpentine or lavender oil. The color is ground with the medium to the consistency of artist's oil paint, using a palette knife on a frosted glass slab. Colors containing gold, such as ruby, maroon, and rose pink, require longer grinding than others. The paint can be thinned with turpentine for spraying. It is best to mix only as much color as will be used at a given time, as it will dry out. The workable period can be extended by using olive oil as a medium. The colors which come in jars are normally prepared to brushing consistency; the tube colors are somewhat thicker, correct for silkscreen printing. Both can be thinned with turpentine for brushing or spraying.

The glazed surface to be decorated should be clean and free of dust. A design can be sketched with india ink or lithographic (wax) pencil. On matt or semimatt glazes a soft lead pencil can be used, but a slick, glossy glaze will not accept a pencil line unless first wiped with a turpentine-moistened cloth. This leaves a slightly tacky film which, depending on individual preference, may or may not be a desirable painting surface. Neither lithographic pencil nor turpentine should be used in conjunction with the semimoist water-soluble colors.

The colors should be applied in a thin coat. A second or third coat can be applied after the first has dried, but too thick an application can cause blistering in firing. If after firing some areas are found to be unsatisfactory, they can be repainted and the pot refired, but very thick applications built up in successive firings may also cause blistering.

As color tones and relationships are essentially the same before and after firing, precise control is possible. Colors can be intermixed, but here the result may not always be what is expected and combinations should be tested first. The temptation, with so many colors easily available, is to become overly complex or painterly. Best results are usually obtained by restricting the palette to a few colors which can be managed in a clear, straightforward way.

Most commercial colors have a recommended firing temperature of about cone 018, although some have a wider range: from a low of cone 022 to 019 to a high of cone 014 to 010. Some colors from the same supplier may be at their best at slightly different temperatures, and some combinations may require more than one firing, the higher-temperature colors being fired before application of the lower-temperature ones.

LOW-TEMPERATURE GLAZES

Any low-temperature glaze could be used for decoration over a glaze fired at a higher temperature. The wide range of commercially prepared cone 06 to 05 glazes can be utilized for decoration over stoneware or porcelain glazes. These glazes are also excellent for polychrome decoration on unglazed stoneware or porcelain which has been fired to maturity.

The commercial cone 06 to 05 glazes offer a wide range of color and texture from bright, shiny primary colors to flat matt pastels and various speckled, crystal, and opalescent glazes. These glazes are generally a similar color before and after firing, although bright primary colors appear as pastels in the raw state. Some colors can be mixed for intermediate shades, but tests should precede actual use.

The cone 05 glazes must be applied more thickly than overglaze enamels and must be thickened with gum arabic or gum tragacanth to adhere to the nonabsorbent ware. It also helps to heat the piece in strong sunlight or in a warm kiln or over—65° to 93° C. (150° to 200° F.). It may be necessary to build up several layers to achieve a dense, opaque color.

A popular technique in Ming dynasty China involved applied decoration which formed a cloisonné network. After firing the ware unglazed to maturity, polychrome medium-temperature glazes were applied, separated by the cloisons, which kept the glazes from running during application and in firing.

Firing to cone 06 can safely be done in about 5 hours. Bright, smooth, glossy glazes are likely to run on vertical surfaces if only slightly overfired. They should be fired to the minimum temperature at which they will mature. The color of cadmium-selenium reds is fugitive (see Glossary), and contrary to normal firing practice, these glazes must be cooled rapidly from maximum temperature down to dull red heat to keep the color from turning brown or completely disappearing.

Raku covered jar, about 48″ high. Steve and Susan Kemenyffy, U.S.A. An incised design drawn in the damp clay outlines areas of bright-colored low-fire glazes which contrast vividly with unglazed smoky-gray areas.

Luster-painted bowl, 12″ in diameter. Mesopotamia, 10th century. The Metropolitan Museum of Art, Fletcher Fund. The decoration with its delightfully stylized birds is painted entirely in yellow luster over a white tin glaze.

*Drug jar (*albarello*), about 14" high. Spain (Manises), early 15th century. Victoria and Albert Museum. Decorated in cobalt blue and luster, this jar indicates some of the richness and variety of decorative patterns used in Manises.*

LUSTERS

Lusters are applied over a fired glaze in the form of metallic salts, which in a subsequent low-temperature firing (cone 021 to 015) are reduced to a thin film of metal fused onto the surface of the glaze. There are two basic types of luster. The traditional Middle Eastern type requires a smoky reduction firing, while the type most commonly used today is fired in an oxidizing kiln—the reduction of the metallic salts to metals being accomplished by a reducing agent in the mixture.

Lusters can be used as overall coatings, but may tend to look gaudy and cheap (a quality which has in recent years often been intentionally exploited). Lusters are usually more effectively employed as decoration and are perhaps best when used as accent or counterpoint to underglaze, majolica, or overglaze decoration. (Examples of lusters are shown in the color plates.)

Reduction-Fired Lusters. The luster technique is believed to have originated in Egypt where it was used for decoration on glass about 700 to 800 A.D. During the 9th century, pottery with luster decoration was made in Mesopotamia and Egypt, often combining several colors on one piece. The Islamic potters created various shades of red, brown, green, and yellow lusters, but by the beginning of the 10th century the color range had been reduced to brown or yellow monochrome, perhaps because the polychrome lusters were too difficult to control in firing. The luster technique spread to Persia, Syria, and Spain, its popularity in the Islamic world due partially to the religious sanction against the use of gold and silver vessels, although it was rarely used as an overall coating in imitation of metal.

The magnificent Hispano-Moresque dish (shown on the first page of the color section) is essentially Moorish in conception with Arabic tree-of-life and pseudo-Kufic script patterns radiating from a geometric star. On some similar pieces from the same period, the star was replaced with the coat of arms of the family for which it was made. Although luster is here used essentially as a delicate secondary embellishment of the bold basic design in cobalt blue, it is equally important in the total impact of the piece.

Perhaps the most magnificent achievements in the luster technique are the 14th and 15th century Hispano-Moresque wares. Luster was produced in Spain as early as the 13th century in Málaga and other Andalusian centers, the technique probably having been brought by migrating Iranian potters. By the end of the 14th century, Valencia (reconquered by the Christians in 1238) had superseded Málaga as the major lusterware center, although the Valencian luster was often referred to as *obra de Malica*. Muslim and Christian craftsmen worked side by side in the Valencian potteries, which resulted in a wonderful fusion of Moorish and Gothic styles. Throughout the 15th century, the lusterware of Manises (a suburb of Valencia) was the most sophisticated and sought-after pottery in Europe.

The oldest record of materials and processes for producing lusters is included in a book written in 1301 by Abu'l-Qasim, a member of a famous pottery family from the Persian pottery center, Kashan. Unfortunately some of the materials mentioned cannot be identified with certainty, and the text is sometimes unclear or contradictory.

The Italian potter Cipriano Piccolpasso included a description of the luster technique in his famous three-volume treatise *Arte del Vasaro* (published around 1550). From Spain we have accounts of the potters of Muel (1586), Alcora (1749 and 1765), and clearest, and most complete, the head of the potters guild of Manises (1785). The materials specified in these accounts vary, but in all the basic principle is the same. Copper and silver, either as metals or metallic salts, are calcined and ground with red ochre and mixed with vinegar.

The Manises formula from 1785 calls for 3 ounces copper, one silver peseta, 3 ounces sulphur, and 12 ounces red ochre. The copper, silver, and sulphur were heated in a crucible until the sulphur was consumed. When cool, it was ground very fine with the red ochre, 36 ounces of the sediment from the tub of water in which the pottery had been cleaned after the luster firing, and enough water to make a paste, which was spread on the inside walls of a large crucible and heated for 6 hours in the kiln during a bisque firing. It was then scraped out and ground for a couple of hours with vinegar.

The mixture was applied to fired glazed surfaces with brushes and quill or reed pens. The ware was then refired in an updraft kiln using oak or shrubs such as furze or rosemary for fuel. The tin-lead glaze matured at about 800° C. (1472° F. or cone 015). The luster was fired to about 600° C. (1112° F. or cone 021). A smoky, heavily reducing atmosphere in the luster firing reduced the metallic oxides to a

Hispano-Moresque dish, 17" in diameter. Spain, Manises, about 1430 A.D. Victoria and Albert Museum. The complex, but bold decoration is in cobalt blue and reddish gold luster.

Reverse of above. The undersides of the 15th-century Manises dishes are usually decorated with exceptionally vigorous and dynamic brushwork, often featuring heraldic beasts such as this griffin.

Luster-painted dish. Italy (Deruta), 1520–25 A.D. Victoria and Albert Museum. Luster decoration was first used in Italy at Deruta about 1501. This piece is decorated in Majolica blue and gold luster on a white tin glaze.

Luster-painted jar. Iraq, mid-9th century. Art Institute, Chicago. The decoration is painted in dark-brown and golden-brown lusters.

thin metal film fused onto the glaze. The blackened pigment left on the surface was removed by washing the piece in a tub of water or rubbing it with moist earth to reveal the gleaming luster.

Similar luster formulas and methods of preparing them, and similar kilns, fuel, and firing procedures are still used by some potteries in Manises. The 1785 formula is followed almost exactly by one modern version which calls for, by weight: copper 91.80, silver 5.05, sulphur 91.80, red ochre 367.20. This is not, however, the wonderfully subtle, iridescent 15th-century luster with its elusive reflections of blue, red, purple, lavender, green, silver, gold, or bronze, but the brighter, more metallic, coppery luster with little or no iridescence which began to appear in the 16th century. The earlier luster probably contained a high proportion of silver and the glaze over which it was applied more tin, but other variables, such as firing procedure, may have contributed to the difference.

Another modern Manises formula calls for grinding together and calcining the sulphides of copper and silver, then mixing them with red ochre and vinegar. Actually, metallic salts or carbonates can simply be mixed with ochre and water to form a thin paste which needs sieving only through a 60-mesh screen to be ready for painting on glazed ware. Red ochre is the traditional vehicle, but other ferrous earths such as yellow ochre, burnt umber, or burnt sienna may be used. Vinegar, wine, or a gum-tragacanth solution, instead of water, provides better adhesion of the luster pigment to the ware before firing.

Reduced lusters are notoriously unpredictable as they are radically affected by small differences in composition, firing, and glaze over which they are applied. Generally copper carbonate or copper sulphate produces red, reddish gold, or coppery luster; silver carbonate or silver nitrate produces ivory or yellow; bismuth trioxide or bismuth subnitrate produces iridescence in combination with other metals. Mercury sulphide in small amounts tends to intensify colors. Two metals are often combined, as in the Spanish lusters. The ratio of vehicle to metallic salts may range from 1 to 1 to as high as 5 to 1.

In Spain and the Middle East, luster was most often applied over an opaque white tin-lead glaze, although transparent glazes were also used and a magnificently lush, yet subtly elusive quality was obtained when luster was applied over a deep-turquoise alkaline glaze.

Although reduced lusters are most often used over tin-lead glazes maturing between cone 015 and 02, they may be used over other types of glazes, but it must be remembered that the composition of the glaze itself will affect the color and quality of the luster. To insure a durable bond between the glaze and the luster film, the glaze should just begin to melt at the luster temperature.

The luster firing should proceed with a normal oxidation atmosphere up to dull red heat at which time heavy reduction is begun and maintained for 30 minutes to one hour until the required temperature is reached, usually cone 021 to 018 (about 614° to 717° C., 1137° to 1323° F.).

The damper, firemouth, and stoking ports of a wood-burning kiln can be closed to create dense black clouds of smoke in the firing chamber. The damper and primary air supply of a gas- or oil-fired kiln can be closed, but it may still be necessary to introduce additional combustible material such as sawdust or small pieces of wood to attain a sufficiently smoky atmosphere. Increase or even maintenance of temperature may require alternate periods of heavy and light smoking. Some potters recommend continuing heavy reduction during cooling until the kiln is dark. When removed from the kiln the ware will be blackened by the heavy reduction and requires washing or possibly rubbing with fine, moist powdered clay to reveal the luster.

Detailed firing schedules and formulas for luster glazes and pigments can be found in the book entitled *Glazes for Special Effects* by Herbert Sanders.

Oxidation Lusters. Lusters produced in oxidation firing, although rarely comparable in subtlety and richness to successful reduction fired lusters, are simple to use and much more predictable and dependable. The mixtures are composed of metallic salts and resin with oil of turpentine or oil of lavender as a medium. They are fired in an oxidizing kiln to a low temperature, usually about cone 021 to 018 (about 614° to 717° C.), although some lusters may be fired as high as cone 015. The reductions of the metallic salts is accomplished by carbon released by the combustion of the resin and oil, which burn out in the firing, leaving a bright film of metal on the glazed surface.

Prepared, ready-to-use lusters are available from various manufacturers in a range of iridescent colors including yellow, orange, pink, red, chartreuse, green, blue, turquoise, purple, and pearl. Liquid bright gold and platinum are not iridescent but develop brilliant, reflective metallic surfaces. Iridescence can be achieved by applying a thin coat of opal or pearl luster over the fired gold or platinum. Large areas, even entire pots, can be covered with a flawless gold or platinum surface by applying one or two thin, even coats. Some unevenness in application smooths out in the firing. Burnish gold or Roman gold, available in liquid or paste form, must be polished with fine burnishing sand after firing to develop a sheen. It has a softer, warmer character than bright gold.

Lusters are only as shiny as the glaze over which they are applied and so are effective only over glossy glazes. One luster can be used over another, but there must be a firing between. Transparent mother-of-pearl luster is often used over other lusters, especially gold or platinum. Lusters may be sprayed, but are usually applied with soft camel-hair brushes. To avoid contamination, these brushes should be used only for luster, and it is best to have separate brushes for different colors. Brushes should be carefully cleaned in denatured alcohol, then oil of lavender, and stored in a dust-free container. Unlike overglaze enamels, most lusters appear brown before firing and cannot generally be intermixed except for different shades of the same color. Finely detailed linear decoration can be done with quill, reed, or steel pens. There is even a commercially produced pen for drawing with liquid gold.

Before applying lusters, the glazed surface should be cleaned with a cloth dampened with alcohol, as any dust or oil will cause spots in the fired luster. Commercial lusters must be applied in a thin, even film. If too thin, the luster will be dull, if too thick, it may blister or even flake off. Luster solutions which are too thick are normally thinned with oil of lavender, often sold as luster essence or gold essence.

Luster-decorated ware must be stored in a dust-free place until fired, as dust on the raw luster causes specking. Any unwanted smudges of luster can easily be removed with alcohol. After firing, luster can be removed with a gold eraser or with liquid rust remover.

Oxidation lusters can be fired to cone 020 to 018 in 2 to 3 hours. A small electric kiln is ideal. The kiln must be well ventilated up to about 430°C. (806°F.) to allow fumes and smoke from the volatile oils to escape. Ware should not be stacked too closely, especially if large areas are lustered. The kiln should be turned off as soon as the desired temperature is reached to avoid overfiring the luster.

SPECIALIZED TECHNIQUES

Airbrushed, screen-printed, and deal decoration have until recent years been generally rejected by artist potters as slick and commercial—inappropriate for handcrafted ceramics. Now more and more potters are experimenting with these techniques, and although most of this work is satirical in nature, often mocking the techniques themselves, an appreciation of their creative potential is growing.

SPRAYERS

Properly thinned slips, colorants, or glazes can be applied by spraying on raw or bisque-fired clay or over unfired glaze. Overglaze colors or lusters can be sprayed over fired glazes. Spraying can create subtle shaded effects unobtainable by other means.

If spraying is used as the basic means of applying glazes to large numbers of pots, a regular spray gun, air compressor, and ventilated spray booth are required, but for decoration, beautiful results can be achieved with a simple hand-pumped sprayer (such as those used for insecticides). A removable wide-mouth cup is best as this makes it easier to keep the sprayer clean and to correct clogging when it occurs.

Aerosol sprayers, consisting of a spray unit, replaceable propellant can, and glass jar for colorant, slip or glaze, are compact, convenient, and cheap, but refill propellant cans are rather expensive.

AIRBRUSH

The most subtle gradations and precise control are obtainable with an airbrush, a tool long used by commercial artists and designers. An airbrush is simply a very small spray gun which looks rather like a clumsy fountain pen and is held in the same way as a pen. Airbrushes are normally fitted with a small color cup which requires frequent refilling, but some models can be fitted with larger glass or plastic jars.

The air supply comes from a compressor or carbon-dioxide cylinders. A good compressor is more expensive initially but may be more economical in the long run. Twenty-pound CO_2 cylinders (as used in soda fountains) are silent, clean, and have no moving parts to wear out.

Some airbrushes have separate air and color controls, allowing the color adjustment to be preset, while others have a single double-action lever which controls both air and color. An in-out movement controls air while a back-and-forth movement controls the color. This double-action type is more flexible and versatile as the amount of color being sprayed can be infinitely regulated during painting.

Effective use of the airbrush requires skillful coordination of four separate factors: the air control, amount of color released, distance of

"Made in U.S.A. #23," slab-built, oxidation stoneware plate, silkscreen printed, airbrushed underglaze. Stamped decoration, underglaze pencil, 21" in diameter. Les Lawrence, U.S.A.

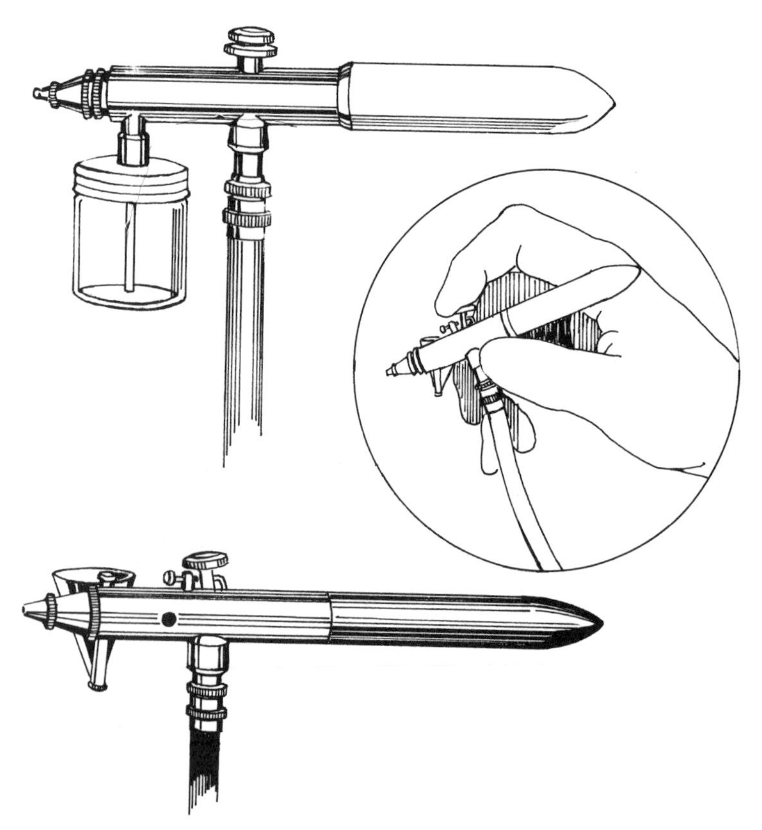

Airbrushes: (top) Wold single-action with glass jar for color (bottom) Thayer and Chandler double-action with color cup.

Porcelain envelope box, 15½" high. Susanne Stephenson, U.S.A. Fired to stoneware temperature cone 10 and refired at cone 06, with airbrushed red, red-orange, and turquoise and white stripes. Refired at cone 017 with gold luster.

the airbrush from the surface being sprayed, and the direction and speed of the movement of the airbrush. Considerable practice may be necessary to develop the required synchronization, and it is a good idea to practice on sheets of newsprint to gain confidence and smoothness before attempting to work on actual pots. Heavy application causing wet spots should be avoided; dense color should be built up in several layers. Airbrush decoration is characterized by soft, fuzzy edges and gentle gradations and blending of colors, but hard edges can be introduced by using stencils or liquid latex. Airbrush decoration is often most effective when combined with other techniques such as brushwork or sgraffito.

The airbrush can be used for decorating on raw or bisqued clay or over raw or fired glaze. Slips, glazes, or colorants for airbrush use must be very finely ground and sieved, as any coarse particle will clog the delicate mechanism. The airbrush should be cleaned by spraying clean water through it and dryed by spraying only air through it.

SCREEN PRINTING

The screen-printing process, developed in the late 19th century, is a type of stencil printing with which complex and detailed designs or images can be printed. The stencil is affixed to or embedded in thin, finely woven silk or synthetic fabric, which has been tightly and evenly stretched over a wood frame. The printing medium is forced by a rubber squeegee through the unblocked areas of the screen mesh and is deposited in a thin layer on the receiving surface. Numerous sophisticated materials, techniques, and processes have been developed for commercial screen printing. Many of these require only simple basic equipment and can be used in pottery decoration.

Designs can be printed with slips or underglaze pigments directly onto soft clay slabs or onto leatherhard or bisque-fired pots, provided the surface is flat. Overglaze colorants can be printed onto fired glaze surfaces, but it is usually better to print decals which can easily be adhered to both flat and irregular surfaces. Decals can also be printed in underglaze colors and applied to raw or bisque ware.

There are five basic types of stencils for screen printing: blockout, resist, paper, lacquer film, and photographic, each with advantages and limitations and each with its own unique character. The first three have limited appeal as pottery decoration techniques, as similar effects can be created directly on individual pots with the brushwork, wax resist, and paper stencil techniques discussed in Chapter 6. The lacquer film and photostencil, however, offer not only a convenient means of multiple duplication, but the potential for printing designs or images difficult or impossible to achieve by other means.

Blockout Stencils. Areas not to print are blocked out with a hard-drying liquid, usually water-soluble fish-type glue or lacquer. Glue stencils are easily cleaned from the screen mesh with water, but cannot be used with water-based printing media such as slip. Lacquer stencils are more durable, can be used with oil- or water-based colors, and can be removed from the screen with lacquer thinner.

Resist Stencils. This is actually a variation of the blockout method in which the blockout fluid is applied over a resist material, masking the areas which are to print. When the blockout fluid has dried, the resist is removed, leaving those areas open. Lithographic tusche in liquid or crayon form is used as a resist for glue. When the glue has dried, the tusche is dissolved with kerosene or turpentine. Wax emulsion (removed with hot water) or liquid latex can be used as resists for lacquer.

Paper Stencils. Paper stencils are simple and quick to make and can produce clear, sharp prints, but they are not durable and are not suitable for use with water-based printing media. They are normally adhered to the underside of the screen by the printing medium itself. Printing must be done immediately after adhering, and the screen cannot be cleaned without ruining the stencil.

Lacquer-Film Stencils. Very precise, cleanly cut, finely detailed stencils can be made with lacquer film, a thick layer of colored lacquer on a transparent paper or plastic backing. The design is cut through the lacquer (not the backing), and the areas to print are stripped off. The stencil with backing intact is affixed to the underside of the screen with adhering fluid (a type of lacquer thinner). When the stencil is dry, the backing is peeled off. Lacquer-film stencils are very durable and can be used with oil-or water-based printing media. To reclaim the screen, the stencil is removed with lacquer thinner. The laminated film is available in three weights; the thicker stencils are used when a heavy deposit of color is desired, as when printing with slip.

Stoneware plate. Petr Svodboda, Czechoslovakia. Stencils and overlapping, subtly contrasting glazes are used to create quite simple undulating patterns.

"One-Half of the All American Comedy Team," slip-cast earthenware, commercial photodecals. Jonathan Kaplan, U.S.A.

The transparent film can be placed over a drawing of the design for tracecutting. The most common tool is a simple stencil knife with fixed or interchangeable blades. The blade must be kept very sharp so that the film is easily cut with minimum pressure to obtain clean, sharp stencils. Fine lines can be cut and stripped in one operation with scooper cutters, which are similar to the wire loop sgraffito tools but with very sharp cutting edges. Other special tools include swivel-bladed knives, adjustable twin-bladed knives for parallel lines, and compass cutters.

Photographic Stencils. Photographic stencils are made using a photosensitive gelatin emulsion which hardens and becomes water insoluble when exposed to light. The pattern in the stencil is created by partially masking the emulsion-coated surface from the light source, usually accomplished with a transparent positive (an opaque design or image on a transparent surface, usually acetate). This may be drawn, painted, or photographically printed. With proper exposure the unprotected emulsion is hardened, while the protected areas remain soft and are easily washed out with a warm-water spray. The emulsion can also be masked with cut stencils of opaque materials or actual physical objects, such as string, coarse fabrics, doilies, or metal screens or grilles.

A handmade positive must be restricted to line technique; that is, it must be either opaque or transparent at any given point. Shading or gray areas can be simulated, as in line engravings, by crosshatching, stippling, etc., or by using commercial overlay sheets available in a wide variety of line, dotted, and hatched patterns.

A photographic positive is made by printing a negative on transparent orthographic film, producing a high-contrast image of opaque and transparent areas. The gray tones of a photograph can be simulated by using a halftone process. A halftone screen interposed between negative and positive breaks up the continuous tones of the negative into a series of tiny dots. The clarity of the print depends on how finely spaced the dots are. Relatively coarse 45- to 85-line halftones will be the least troublesome for screen printing, but finer 100- to 120-line halftones may be desirable for small, detailed overglaze decals.

Making transparent positives photographically requires darkroom equipment, but you can have them made commercially at a reasonable cost from your own artwork or photographs.

There are two basic methods of preparing photographic stencils: the direct method in which the screen itself is coated with the sensitized emulsion, then exposed and washed out, and the indirect or transfer method in which the emulsion is carried on a transparent acetate backing. After exposure, it must be developed in a chemical developing solution, then washed, and immediately adhered to the screen. When dry, the backing is peeled off.

For transferring the positive image to the stencil, satisfactory results can be achieved with simple improvised equipment. The emulsion-coated screen (fabric-side up) or transfer film (emulsion-side down) is placed over a felt or foam-rubber padded backboard. The positive (image-side down) is centered over the screen or film and covered by a sheet of plate glass to insure perfect contact between the positive and the screen or film. An ordinary photoflood reflector bulb or fluorescent tube can be used as the light source. The exposure time may range from 5 to 10 minutes to 20 to 40 minutes, depending on the type of emulsion, the type, intensity, and distance of the light source, and other variables. The correct exposure can only be determined by testing, based on the recommendations of the manufacturer for the particular film or emulsion.

Photo-emulsion stencils do not hold up well when used with water-based printing media. There are special direct-method emulsions for use with water-based inks, but some of these cannot be removed from the screen.

During the last ten years, the use of screen-printed photographic images as pottery decoration has become increasingly popular. Unfortunately, it has most often been used in banal, trite ways, with potters and public fascinated by the mere juxtaposition of a fired photographic image on a ceramic surface. As the novelty wears off it is to be hoped that more creative use of the potential of photographic and other types of screen stencils will be made.

Screen Fabric. Silk is the traditional screen fabric, but nylon, dacron, and polyester screens are becoming increasingly popular. Silk fabrics are classified according to mesh size, those normally used for screen printing ranging from 6xx to 20xx, the higher numbers indicating a finer mesh. A coarse to medium mesh of 8xx to 12xx can be used for printing slips. The 12xx silk has 125 holes per linear inch, an aperture size of .0045″, and an open area of 32%. For printing decals in underglaze or overglaze colors, especially with photographic stencils, a finer 16xx mesh is desirable, while for clear printing of halftone stencils, still finer 18xx to 20xx silk or 220- to 240-mesh nylon may be preferred.

Framed screens can be purchased at art supply stores, but are not difficult to fabricate. Large frames can be made of 2x2 clear pine while 1x2 strips are adequate for smaller ones. Simple butt joints can be used, but mitered, lapped, or rabbet joints are stronger. Corners can be reinforced with angle irons. It is important that the assembled frame lie absolutely flat.

The fabric is tightly stretched and fastened with tacks or staples to the underside of the frame, and the area where the fabric contacts the frame is coated with lacquer or shellac. When dry, the tacked surfaces are covered with strips of paper tape or masking tape. The inside corners where the fabric meets the frame are also sealed with tape to prevent seepage during printing, and the entire frame and taped areas are given one or more coats of varnish or shellac.

The size of the frame must be considerably larger than the actual printing area to allow room at the sides for an ink reservoir. This border area is sealed with tape or blockout fluid. The printing medium (slip, underglaze, or overglaze color of a thick paste consistency) is placed along one side of the screen, then pulled across the screen with a squeegee, forcing color through the unblocked areas. A thick deposit of color results from a light pressure on the squeegee, while a heavy pressure produces a thinner layer. A thicker deposit can be built up by additional passes of the squeegee. Work must proceed rapidly with slip as it dries and clogs the screen, which must then be washed out and dried before printing can continue. This drying can be retarded by adding glycerine to the slip. Oil-based colorants have more satisfactory working qualities and tend to produce sharper images.

Multicolor printing is done by using a different stencil for each color. This requires careful registration, and the screens must be hinged to a baseboard or table with positioning guides for the printing stock (slabs, tiles, decal paper) to insure that each color is printed in proper relation to the others.

DECALS

While silkscreen printing directly on irregular surfaces is difficult or impossible, the design can be printed on decal paper, then easily transferred to the ceramic surface. The design can be printed in underglaze colors for application on raw or bisque ware or in overglaze colors for application on fired glaze surfaces. Porous raw or bisque surfaces must first be coated with a sealer (varnish, acrylic base, or decoupage glue) to provide a slick surface on which the wet decal can be positioned. Commercial decals can be used and are available in thousands of designs. There are companies which will fabricate decals of your designs, but this can be expensive, and printing decals is not difficult. Of course, they can be partially or entirely handpainted—but then why not paint directly on the pot. Screen stencils are printed on ordinary decal paper, and when dry coated with a decal varnish. They are applied like any other decal, and can be stretched to fit irregular surfaces. They must be carefully applied, as any overlapping or poorly adhered areas will burn off in firing.

Detailed information on screen-printing techniques and materials can be found in the references given in the bibliography under screen printing.

Stoneware covered jar, with luster and commercial decals. Tyrone Larson, U.S.A.

SLIP FORMULAS AND COLORANTS

There are innumerable, widely varying white slip or engobe compositions which will produce very similar fired results. There are variations for the purposes of controlling shrinkage to fit different clay bodies in wet, dry, or bisque stages, to adjust firing temperature (although slips have a much wider firing range than most glazes), or to increase opacity of the fired slip or toughness of the raw coating.

Following are some typical compositions for white slips to be applied on wet to damp ware, or on leatherhard ware if not thickly applied. For use on dry or bisque ware, some of the raw clay can be replaced with calcined china clay to reduce shrinkage. In a slip applied on dry ware, raw clay should not exceed 40%, on bisque ware, not more than 25%. Some additional flux may also be required for bisque application.

White slips applied on wet to damp ware and fired at stoneware temperatures are normally composed of four basic ingredients: china clay, ball clay, feldspar, and flint, and are often similar or identical to porcelain bodies. One standard recipe for porcelain or engobe is equal parts of these four.

1. Cone 6–11

China clay	30
Ball clay	20
Feldspar	20
Flint	20
Zircopax	5
Borax	5

2. Cone 6–11

China clay	23
Ball clay	22
Feldspar	20
Flint	30
Borax	5

3. Cone 8–10

China clay	50
Ball clay	15
Cornwall stone	20
Flint	10
Zircopax	5

For lower firing temperatures, nepheline syenite (which has a higher proportion of flux to silica) is often used instead of feldspar, and additional fluxes such as talc, magnesium carbonate, or whiting may be added.

4. Cone 04–6

China clay	25
Ball clay	15
Nepheline syenite	25
Flint	25
Zircopax	5
Borax	5

5. Cone 4

China clay	25
Ball clay	20
Feldspar	17
Flint	30
Whiting	3
Magnesium carbonate	5

The following slip compositions will give satisfactory results over a wide temperature range.

6. Cone 04–9

China clay	25
Ball clay	25
Feldspar	10
Flint	25
Talc	10
Borax	5

7. Cone 2–10

China clay	20
Ball clay	15
Nepheline syenite	30
Flint	20
Talc	5
Zircopax	5
Borax	5

SLIP COLORANTS

Colored slips can be made by adding coloring oxides or commercial stains to a basic white slip. The colorant percentages required are somewhat larger than for glazes. About 10% to 20% of a commercial glaze stain is normally used. Colored slips reveal their full color intensity only when covered by a clear glaze. Some suggestions for slip colorants are given below. Most of these colors are good over a wide temperature range in oxidation or reduction.

Colorant	%	Result
Cobalt carbonate	1–5%	light to dark blue
	2–3%	tan
Red iron oxide	4–10%	light to dark brown
	10–20%	dark brown, iron red
Manganese	6–10%	brown, purple-brown
Chromium oxide	1–5%	green
Nickel oxide	2–5%	gray, tan, gray-green
Copper oxide	3–5%	green, charcoal
Iron chromate	1–5%	light to medium gray
Rutile	6–8%	tan, yellow
Vanadium stain	8–10%	yellow
Cobalt carbonate Red iron oxide	1–2% 2–3%	gray-blue
Cobalt carbonate Red iron oxide Chromium oxide	1% 1–2% ½–1%	turquoise
Cobalt carbonate Red iron oxide Manganese dioxide	1–2% 3–5% 2–3%	black
Illmenite or granular manganese	2–3%	produces specks

MAJOLICA COLORANTS

For application on a raw glaze surface, coloring oxides can simply be mixed with water. Some suggested mixtures are listed below. These should be considered approximate as there are many variables, including firing temperature and atmosphere, type of glaze over which the colors are used, and variations in application due to such factors as the absorbency of the dry glaze, loading of the brush, or manner of painting. Add the following colorants in the quantities indicated to ½ cup (4 ounces) of water.

Colorant	Amount	Result
Cobalt carbonate	½–1 teaspoon	blue
Red iron oxide	1–4 teaspoons	tan, red, red-brown
Cobalt carbonate Red iron oxide	½–1 teaspoon ½–1 teaspoon	gray-blue
Cobalt carbonate Chromium oxide	½–1 teaspoon ¼–½ teaspoon	turquoise
Red iron oxide Rutile	1–2 teaspoons 1–2 teaspoons	orange
Manganese dioxide	1 teaspoon	brown, purple-brown
Copper oxide	½–1 teaspoon	green
Red iron oxide Manganese dioxide Cobalt oxide	1 teaspoon ½ teaspoon ½ teaspoon	black

BIBLIOGRAPHY

Periodicals

Ceramic Review, Craftsmen Potters Association of Great Britain, 5 Belsize Lane, London NW3 5AD, England.

Ceramics Monthly, Professional Publications, P.O. Box 4548, Columbus, Ohio 43212.

Craft Horizons, The American Crafts Council, 16 E. 52nd St., New York, N.Y. 10022.

New Zealand Potter, P.O. Box 12-162, Wellington, New Zealand.

Pottery in Australia, Potters Society of Australia, Turramurra, New South Wales.

Pottery Quarterly, Northfield Studio, Northfields, Tring, Herts., England.

Studio Potter, Box 172, Warner, N.H. 03278.

Technical

Binns, Charles F. *The Potter's Craft,* 4th ed. Princeton: Van Nostrand Reinhold, 1967.

Cardew, Michael. *Pioneer Pottery.* London: Longman Group, 1969. New York: St. Martin's, 1971.

Clark, Sir Kenneth. *Practical Pottery and Ceramics.* New York: Viking, and London: Studio Vista, 1964.

Conrad, John W. *Ceramic Formulas: The Complete Compendium.* New York: Macmillan, 1973.

Counts, Charles. *Pottery Workshop.* New York: Macmillan, 1973.

Dodd, A. E. *Dictionary of Ceramics.* New York: Philosophical Library, 1964. London: Butterworth & Co., 1967.

Fournier, Robert. *Illustrated Dictionary of Practical Pottery.* New York: Van Nostrand Reinhold, 1973.

Fraser, Harry. *Electric Kilns.* New York: Watson-Guptill, 1974.

——. *Glazes for the Craft Potter.* New York: Watson-Guptill, and London: Pitman, 1974.

Grebanier, Joseph. *Chinese Stoneware Glazes.* New York: Watson-Guptill, and London: Pitman, 1975.

Green, David. *Pottery Materials and Techniques.* New York: Praeger, 1967.

——. *Understanding Pottery Glazes.* London: Faber and Faber, 1963, and New York: Watson-Guptill, 1973.

Hamilton, David. *Van Nostrand Reinhold Manual of Pottery and Ceramics.* New York: Van Nostrand Reinhold, 1973.

Kriwanek, Franz F. *Keramos.* Dubuque, Iowa: Kendall/Hunt, 1970.

Lakofsky, Charles. *Pottery.* Dubuque, Iowa: Wm. C. Brown Co., 1968.

Lawrence, W. G. *Ceramic Science for the Potter.* Philadelphia: Chilton, 1972.

Leach, Bernard H. *A Potter's Book,* 2nd ed. London: Faber and Faber, 1945, and Levittown, New York: Transatlantic.

Nelson, Glen C. *Ceramics,* 3rd ed. New York: Holt, Rinehart and Winston, 1971.

North, Frederick H. *Ceramics for the Artist Potter.* Reading, Mass.: Addison-Wesley, 1956.

Parmalee, Cullen W. *Ceramic Glazes,* 2nd ed. Chicago: Industrial Publications, 1951.

Rhodes, Daniel. *Clay and Glazes for the Potter,* rev. ed. Philadelphia: Chilton, and London: Pitman, 1973.

——. *Kilns.* Philadelphia: Chilton, 1968, and London: Pitman, 1969.

——. *Stoneware and Porcelain.* Philadelphia: Chilton, 1959, and London: Pitman, 1960.

Rothenberg, Polly. *The Complete Book of Ceramic Art.* New York: Crown, 1972.

Sanders, Herbert H. *Glazes for Special Effects.* New York: Watson-Guptill, 1974.

——. *The World of Japanese Ceramics.* Scranton, Pa.: Kodansha International, 1967.

Shaw, K. *Ceramic Colours and Pottery Decoration.* Barking, Essex, England: Maclaren and Sons, 1968.

Airbrush and Screen Printing Techniques

Anvil, Kenneth. *Serigraphy: Silk Screen Techniques for the Artist.* Englewood Cliffs, N.J.: Prentice-Hall, 1965.

Bartel, Marvin. "Silk Screening with Slip," *Ceramics Monthly,* 3 (1973).

Biegeleisen, J.I. *Screen Printing.* New York: Watson-Guptill, and London: Evans Bros. Ltd., 1971.

Kaplan, Jonathan. "Making Ceramic Decals," *Ceramics Monthly,* 4 (1975):Part I, 18–21; 5 (1975):Part II, 40–44.

Kosloff, Albert. *Photographic Screen Process Printing.* Cincinnati: Signs of the Times Publishing Co., 1968.

Maurello, S. Ralph. *The Complete Airbrush Book.* New York: W. Penn, 1955.

Musacchia, John B. *Airbrush Techniques for Commercial Art,* rev. ed. New York: Van Nostrand Reinhold, 1961.

Schwalbach, Mathilda and James. *Screen Process Printing for the Serigrapher and Textile Designer.* New York: Van Nostrand Reinhold, 1970.

Pottery History

Caiger-Smith, Alan. *Tin Glaze Pottery in Europe and the Islamic World.* London: Faber and Faber, and Atlantic Highlands, N.J.: Humanities Press, 1974.

Cooper, Emmanuel. *A History of Pottery.* New York: Macmillan, and London: St. Martin's, 1972.

Cox, Warren E. *The Book of Pottery and Porcelain.* 2 vols. rev. ed. New York: Crown, 1970.

Haggar, R. *Pottery through the Ages.* London: Methuen, 1959.

Honey, W. B. *Art of the Potter.* London: Faber and Faber, 1955.

Rieth, A. *5000 Jahre Topferscheibe.* Konstanz, West Germany: Jan Thorbecke Verlag, 1960.

Savage, George. *Porcelain Through the Ages.* New York: Penguin, 1954.

Prehistoric and Ancient Pottery

Charleston, Robert J. *Roman Pottery.* London: Faber and Faber, 1955.

Eyles, D. *Pottery in the Ancient World.* London: Doulton, 1950.

Lane, Arthur. *Greek Pottery.* London: Faber and Faber, 1956.

Martinatos, Spyridon. *Crete and Mycenae.* New York: Abrams, 1960.

Noble, Joseph V. *The Techniques of Painted Attic Pottery.* London: Faber and Faber, 1956, and New York: Watson-Guptill, 1965.

Raphael, Max. *Prehistoric Pottery.* New York: Pantheon, 1947.

Far Eastern Pottery

Garner, Sir Harry. *Oriental Blue and White.* London: Faber and Faber, 1964.

Gompertz, G. St. G. M. *Chinese Celadon Wares.* London: Faber and Faber, 1958.

Gray, B. *Early Chinese Pottery and Porcelain.* London: Faber and Faber, 1953.

Griffing, Robert P. *The Art of the Korean Potter.* New York: Asia Society, 1968.

Hobson, R. L. *The Art of the Chinese Potter.* London: Ernest Benn, 1923.

Honey, William B. *Ceramic Art of China.* London: Faber and Faber, 1945.

Hetherington, A. C. *Early Ceramic Wares of China.* London: Ernest Benn, 1922.

Jenyns, Soame. *Japanese Porcelain.* London: Faber and Faber, 1965.

——. *Ming Pottery and Porcelain.* London: Faber and Faber, 1953.

Kidder, J. Edward. *The Birth of Japanese Art.* New York: Praeger, 1964.

——. *Jomon Pottery.* Scranton, Pa.: Kodansha International, 1968.

Leach, Bernard. *Kenzan and His Tradition.* London: Faber and Faber, 1966.

Munsterberg, Hugo. *The Ceramic Art of Japan.* Rutland, Vt.: Tuttle, 1964.

Prodan, Mario. *The Art of the T'ang Potter.* London: Thames and Hudson, 1960.

Rhodes, Daniel. *Tamba Pottery.* Scranton, Pa.: Kodansha International, 1970.

Middle Eastern Pottery

Butler, A. J. *Islamic Pottery.* London: Ernest Benn, 1926.

Hobson, R. L. *A Guide to the Islamic Pottery of the Near and Far East.* London: British Museum, 1932.

Lane, Arthur. *Early Islamic Pottery.* London: Faber and Faber, 1958.

——. *Later Islamic Pottery.* London: Faber and Faber, 1957.

Hetjens Museum. *Islamische Keramik.* Dusseldorf: Hetjens Museum, 1973.

Wilkinson, Charles K. *Iranian Ceramics.* New York: Abrams, 1963.

European Pottery

Conti, Giovanni. *L'Arte della Maiolica in Italia.* Milan: Bramante Editrice, 1973.

Cooper, R. G. *English Slipware Dishes.* London: Tiranti, 1968.

Frothingham, Alice W. *Lustreware of Spain.* New York: Hispanic Society of America, 1951.

Gonzalez-Marti, Manuel. *Ceramica del Levante Español; siglos medievales,* vol. I; Loza Barcelona, Madrid, etc.: Editorial Labor, 1944, 1952.

Honey, William B. *European Ceramic Art* (2 vols.). London: Faber and Faber, and New York: Van Nostrand Reinhold, 1949.

Koetschau, Karl. *Rheinisches Steinzeug.* Munich: Kurt Wolff Verlag, 1923.

Rackham, Bernard. *Italian Majolica.* London: Faber and Faber, 1952.

Rackham, B., and H. Read. *English Pottery.* London: Ernest Benn, 1924.

Reineking-von Bock, Gisela. *Steinzeug.* Cologne: Kunstgewerbemuseum der Stadt Köln, 1971.

American Pottery

Anton, Ferdinand, and Frederick J. Dockstader. *Pre-Columbian Art.* New York: Abrams, 1968.

Bushnell, G. H. S. *Ancient Arts of the Americas.* New York: Praeger, 1965.

——, and A. Digby. *Ancient American Pottery.* London: Faber and Faber, 1955.

Dockstader, Frederick J. *Indian Art in South America.* Greenwich, Conn.: New York Graphic Society, 1967.

Guilland, Harold F. *Early American Folk Pottery.* Philadelphia: Chilton, 1971.

Powell, Elizabeth A. *Pennsylvania Pottery: Tools and Processes.* Doylestown, Pa.: Bucks County Historical Society, 1972.

Webster, Donald B. *Decorated Stoneware Pottery of North America.* Rutland, Vermont: Tuttle, 1970.

Contemporary Pottery

Casson, Michael. *Pottery in Britain Today.* London: Tiranti, and Levittown, New York: Transatlantic Press, 1967.

Coyne, John (ed.). *Penland School of Crafts Book of Pottery.* New York: Bobbs-Merrill, 1975.

Hettes, Karel, and Rada, Pravoslav. *Modern Ceramics.* London: Spring Books, 1965.

Lewenstein, Eileen, and Cooper, Emmanuel. *New Ceramics.* New York: Van Nostrand Reinhold, 1974.

Miscellaneous

Christie, Archibald H. *Pattern Design.* New York: Dover, 1969.

Leach, Bernard. *A Potter in Japan.* London: Faber and Faber, 1960.

——. *Hamada, Potter.* Scranton, Pa.: Kodansha International, 1975.

——. *The Potter's Challenge.* New York: Dutton, 1975.

Piccolpasso, Cipriano. *The Three Books of the Potter's Art.* Translated and edited by Rackham, B. and Van de Put. London: Victoria and Albert Museum, 1934.

Speltz, Alexander. *The Styles of Ornament.* New York: Dover, 1959.

Yee, Chiang. *Chinese Calligraphy.* Cambridge, Mass.: Harvard University Press, 1973.

GLOSSARY/INDEX

Numbers in italic refer to illustrations